D1106256

8^{50}

Jacks D/8

❧ NATURE'S MESSAGES

Nature's Messages

A Book of Wilderness Wisdom

By SAM CAMPBELL

RAND M^{c}NALLY & COMPANY

New York · CHICAGO · San Francisco

LILLIAN'S
Help Yourself Bookshelf
124 S. Sherman Street
Denver 9, Colorado

COPYRIGHT 1952 BY RAND MᶜNALLY & COMPANY.
COPYRIGHT 1952 UNDER INTERNATIONAL COPYRIGHT
UNION BY RAND MᶜNALLY & COMPANY.
ALL RIGHTS RESERVED.

First Printing, September, 1952

Library of Congress Card Catalog Number: 52-10417

LITHOGRAPHED AND BOUND IN THE UNITED STATES OF AMERICA
BY RAND MᶜNALLY & COMPANY

To my mother

CONTENTS

CONTENTS

To him who in the love of Nature holds
Communion with her visible forms, she speaks
A various language; for his gayer hours
She has a voice of gladness, and a smile
And eloquence of beauty, and she glides
Into his darker musings, with a mild
And healing sympathy, that steals away
Their sharpness, ere he is aware.

—BRYANT, "Thanatopsis"

Soft silence, strong faith, restful patience, and peace of mind reign when we dwell in blessed sylvan mansions.

A MESSAGE
FROM THE AUTHOR

THE Sanctuary of Wegimind is my forest home—a few
hundred tree-covered acres lying within the Nicolet
National Forest in northern Wisconsin. It is a simple,
natural woodland, unembellished with landscaping and
elaborate human planning. There are trails that thread
their way through legions of trees—hemlock, pine,
spruce, cedar, balsam, maple, oak, and birch—and minor
roads have been developed as an aid to fire control;
otherwise nature is left free to run her course.

Wegimind is the Ojibway word for "mother." The
name "Sanctuary of Wegimind" was selected to honor
the memory of my serene, thoughtful, spiritually
minded mother whose love of nature always has been
an inspiration to me. It was she who first introduced
me to the woods; and it was she who made me realize
that animal wildness is but a form of fear, and that kindness and patience will reveal a fine phase of animal
nature hidden to cruel or misunderstanding treatment.

11

In the sylvan mansions of the Sanctuary live many forest folk—bear, wolf, coyote, wildcat, deer, beaver, otter, and smaller creatures. My primary purpose in establishing this woodland home was to carry on my study of these living animals. To create an atmosphere favorable to this study, the area was closed to hunting and trapping. Opportunity followed to gain the friendship of many wild creatures, thereby to get a clearer understanding of their characters and intelligence.

While seeking the secrets of nature I have watched the salutary effects of stillness and peace on human hearts and minds. I have seen the overpowering beauty of dawns and sunsets reach into troubled breasts and heal hurts that were thought beyond medicine and philosophy. And I have seen those burdened with grief take on the silence of the forest aisles until they could hear that still, small voice which lifts hope and faith with wordless assurance.

Our woodland acres are still dedicated to the study of forest creatures, but I realize this is but a means to an end. In NATURE'S MESSAGES I have endeavored to record what this way of living really means to the mind of man.

SAM CAMPBELL

✑ NATURE'S MESSAGES

The warm, moist magic
of springtime touches
the earth, and the earth
smiles back with flowers.
What sly sirens these blossoms
are as they coyly catch
our eyes with their beauty
and make us strive to know
their secrets!

ঙ্গ SPRING

SPRING is flowing into the north country!

Mystery and magic are abroad in the forest world today. A few hours back on the trail of time the woods stood brown, gaunt, inert. Tangled masses of last summer's ferns carpeted hillsides; layers of leaves, matted and somber, covered the forest floor; and nature looked as if she intended to abandon all thought of growth. Trees seemed content with their barren branches, leftover snowdrifts rested in shaded hollows, and a huge area of ice floated sullenly in the center of our lake.

But today the south wind blows and the sun is strong and warm. Strange things are happening. Wavelets are wearing away the margins of the ice field, tiny rivulets are running from secluded snowdrifts. Aspen trunks are turning from gray to green, the tips of twigs are swelling. Fingers of infant plants are reaching up from the earth. An awakened spirit of growth rules the woods—spring is flowing into the north country!

I know of no more accurate way to describe the coming of this season than as a flow. It is as though some measureless reservoir of the waters of life opens its gates, and its floods, invisible and omnipotent, deluge the world, calling all things to new living beauty.

I search for a comparable advent. Then I recall the day I stood with some friends at the summit of Mount Tamalpais on San Francisco Bay and witnessed a most strange phenomenon.

It was clear and sunny when we reached the top. Below us was the protected little valley in which grow the Muir Woods, preserved in fitting tribute to the memory of a peaceful soul. To the south we could see the great city and west the endless green waters of the Pacific Ocean. We could see a sailing ship approaching the Golden Gate and, with the aid of strong glasses, could make out her sails, masts, and the foam at her bow as she plunged through the ocean swells.

Then one of the party called attention to an object on the far horizon. A great bank of fog was moving ponderously and irresistibly toward the land. In appearance it suggested a mammoth wall of water suddenly released from some hidden source—an ocean covering an ocean. So real did it appear that we shuddered as the advancing wall enveloped the sailing ship, and we fancied we could see an inverted whirlpool as the boat was caught up in the seething eddies of mist. The illusion was so convincing that it was difficult for us to realize that to the seamen aboard this ship it merely meant running into a fog bank—an experience often repeated and for which they were ably prepared.

The great, ghostly mist-ocean rolled on unhesitatingly upon the land. It flooded the foothills and poured into the valleys. The city vanished beneath its white waves. It splashed vehemently against the mountain below us, whirling and swirling about trees and rocks. The deep silence that attended its advance seemed due to our own sudden deafness. In a remarkably short time the ocean of fog ruled the world, and we stood on a tiny island—the only land above the surface of a newborn sea. It seemed to us that we had looked upon the coming of a new element into the universe.

Often I think of this experience as a symbol of the flow of spring into the forest. Yet the magic waters of spring are not only silent in their advance, but invisible as well. We never see them—only the results of their coming.

How they transform the Sanctuary of Wegimind! They flow upon the snows, and the white blanket of winter melts to a memory. Ice vanishes from the lakes. The unseen waves carry on their crests hordes of migratory birds whose hearts drink deeply of the elixir and break forth with songs of love. Under this divine deluge the sleeping earth awakes, pregnant with life. Spring beauties join hands with sweet-smelling arbutus. The magic waters wash the hillsides and myriad ferns raise their delicate heads; Christmas vine creeps timidly over decaying logs; ground pine tips each tiny branch with new growth. The mystic waves wash the trunks of trees and lichens blush green with life; little leaflets open their eyes to look upon the world.

Flowing lightly upon woodland waters, these flood tides of spring draw forth from pond bottom the water lily, the oddly shaped arum, and the offensively named pickerelweed. They beckon the marsh marigold from obscurity, awaken wild iris from a marshy bed, brighten wintergreen, and stir the lady-slipper from its slumbers. They wash sleep from the eyes of the bear, raccoon, and skunk, calling them all from winter's lethargy. Under their silent spell the great buck grows his antlers anew and the mother doe busies herself with caring for her little speckled fawn.

As though an overflow from the fountain of youth, the waters of spring call forth luster, brilliance, and animation from all nature and, to nature lovers, reveal a glorious world which savors of new creation. Nor is their influence limited to the realm of fauna and flora. They polish skies, set waves to dancing, animate singing streams, and add brilliance to sun, moon, and stars. And knowing no limit or barrier, they flow into the heart of man—washing it of harbored ills, refreshing hope, cleansing faith, renewing strength and purpose.

Many and beautiful are the gifts of spring, not the least of which is the silent suggestion of the omnipotence of life. A deep thinker once wrote, "It is not merely the multiplicity of tints, the gladness of tone, or the balminess of the air which delight in the spring;

A wise and devoted
Canadian goose mother
schools her feathered brood
in the ways of the forest.
Contrary to popular proverb,
the goose is not silly
but one of the most intelligent
creatures ever to dwell
in nature's vast household.

it is the still consecrated spirit of hope, the prophecy of happy days yet to come; the endless variety of nature, with presentiments of eternal flowers which never shall fade, and sympathy with the blessedness of the ever-developing world."

Joyous though we find the other seasons of the year, spring in its fine symbolism climaxes human experience. But often in my buoyant happiness at this season I have been brought to pause by thoughts of a wisdom which some day I hope to accept fully. Says this reasoning: "If spring is such a supreme event, let me not forget that all the rest of the year prepared its coming. There was something of spring in the summer gone by, something of it in the autumn when countless leaves fluttered to earth to make room for the legions to come. There was something of spring in the snows that covered the forest, moistening the ground and blanketing the seedling. It is the year which makes the spring, not spring which makes the year—all seasons truly join hands to reflect the glories of creation."

Could not cultivated vision see this so clearly that joy would encompass the calendar and the world be revealed as perpetually in the arms of spring? I think it could, and out of this arise a happiness that is never nipped by frost. And perhaps we could carry forward this affirmation until we come to understand that the winter months of human affairs, chilled with friendlessness, darkened with drifts of difficulties, long of shadows and short of light, but serve as a trial of our faith and are followed by a springtime of resurrection, the absolute certainty of which is sufficient to fill the coldest hours with warm joy borrowed from the future.

The silent flood waters of spring are a symbol not so much of birth as of life never ending.

Feathered folk come and go, decking trees with their homes, filling the air with song, uplifting thought.

⋙ RENDEZVOUS

ONE of the inexplicable things in nature, at least to our present limited understanding, is the strange faculty of instinct, found in both animals and men. In men instinct has been smothered and lost in self-consciousness and, with questionable benefit at times, compromised with reasoning; in domesticated animals too we see evidence that some of that unconscious guidance is falling away as the creatures are drawn more and more into man's way of living. Yet instinct, in purpose, seems to be wholly good. It suggests a ray of wisdom and divine guidance, shining faintly through the mist of matter and dimly discerned by dull thoughts.

Francis Bacon wrote, "Who taught the parrot his 'Welcome?' Who taught the raven in a drought to throw pebbles into a hollow tree where she espied water, that the water might rise so as she might come to it? Who taught the bee to sail through such a vast sea of air, and to find the way from a flower in a field to her

23

hive? Who taught the ant to bite every grain of corn that she burieth in her hill, lest it should take root and grow?"

To his thoughts might be added other questions: Whence came the wisdom that leads the beaver to build his dam, create his pond, and build his remarkable home? What is it that leads the hibernators to store either food or fat in preparation for a winter they have never seen? What sends the tiny feathered traveler from one continent to another with such definite purpose that the two terminals of the journey may be single trees and a previously used nest?

In June of each year I have a rendezvous with one whom I pray instinct shall never fail as a guide. The meeting place is at Vanishing Lake, some distance back of the Sanctuary in the forest. It is a lovely spot for a rendezvous—and experience leads me to picture it during the Junes to come.

It will be a warm day, the polished fingertips of balsam twigs reaching forth into the morning, star-flowers smiling up from a bed of pine needles, and marsh marigolds making the lowlands look as if spattered with sunshine. There will be lazy white clouds floating barely out of reach of the spruce tops, a sky of indescribable blue, the lake vivid with reflections of countless miracles. Aspen trees will be lush green with tender leaflets, their trunks shining with new life. Martins, imbued with spring, will be coasting, diving, clucking, and calling. The modest Christmas vine will be creeping out among sprouting ferns; and arbutus, having cast its sweet breath to heaven, will be retiring to prepare for another June. Maple leaves will be spreading, daintily colored, as if practicing for the brilliant carnival of the autumn; birches will be white in new accouterment, their delicate leaves dancing in each forest breeze.

Yes, on some June morning all these things will tell me the hour is at hand, and I shall go down Vanishing Lake Trail to keep my rendezvous.

Chipmunks will dart through the underbrush at my side, and perhaps one or two of the most intimate climb upon me. Red squirrels will chatter at me from the trees overhead, blue jays call to me from out of the sky; a belted kingfisher will dive into the water as I pass the tarn and rise chattering to his perch on a green bough. I shall be light of heart and free of care, knowing beyond all argument that the happy hour has come—knowing in a way that passes the powers of reasoning.

Oh, I know well how it will seem to climb that last hill, beyond which lies Vanishing Lake. I know the spot at which I shall pause to catch my first glimpse of that lovely little bit of water. I shall stand with my hand upon the trunk of a slender young red pine and look out through a leafy framework on a small portion of the tiny lake. Perhaps a deer will be drinking at the water's edge. Sphagnum moss, which is slowly covering the lake, will be brilliant with new growth, and lowland spruce that grow in the moss, tipped with light, bright green.

Impatience and excitement will finally break this pause, and I shall hurry on down the trail to an old log upon which I shall sit and, with a stump for a back rest, await the one who is to come.

Perhaps this coming will not be at once. I shall have time to calm myself, to watch an old bald eagle sailing through the air, to see a muskrat swim the lake, to hear a rabbit nose his way through the brush. But I know the one whom I seek will not fail me. The instinct that has led me here this hour has guided this lovely one nearly nine thousand miles through unmarked air trails, even to another continent and back.

Then the sacred moment will come. All the forest will take on a deeper silence, and out of the stillness will come the clear bell-like song of the olive-backed thrush. I shall catch my breath, my heart will pound in excitement, but I shall force calmness that I may hear again the song supreme. It will start low, rising in both tone and volume through a series of perfectly rhythmed musical semicircles, pausing briefly between the phrases to dwell beautifully on dual tones.

For an hour I shall listen, answering only with my thoughts. I shall not seek the singer; our rendezvous is with love and beauty, not a personal appointment. And this meeting is inwardly compelled, for as I return north from circling about in the world, so does the songster, and instinct guides us both back to this valley.

The song will cease and, as I climb the hill to return to the Sanctuary that day, I shall breathe forth a prayer of gratitude—gratitude that in highly developed instinct is the unquestionable evidence of Supreme Intelligence ruling the universe.

While I am aware of the tremendous value of reasoning in the world, I think that it is often colored with selfishness, greed, and egotism which render it not true reasoning at all. It seems to me that the more important things are those which are whispered to us from within, and the constructive function of reasoning is to make these things a part of consciousness through definite acceptance of them.

There are those grand instincts in the consciousness of man which are glorious in their promise, yet which the world would crucify and destroy with its shallow reasoning if it could. Perhaps the greatest sermon preached by solitude in the green cathedral is, "Listen to the still, small voice within and fear not to accept the wonders of divine instinct and intuition."

When love and kindness span the gap between the world
of wild creatures and our own, adventure awaits us.

BOBBIE BIDES A WEE

It was a foreboding world on which Bobbie, the fawn, looked that early spring day on which he was born. His big, blinking eyes stared in wonderment at the towering pine trees as he lay trying to collect his thoughts. His lovely speckled coat made him almost indistinguishable on the sun-flecked forest floor.

Most everything about him was as he had instinctively expected—the trees, the sky, the earth, his mother standing guard over him. And yet there was *something*, something that impressed him as both unnatural and unpleasant. The air of the northern forest, which should have been pine scented and invigorating, was laden with a pungent odor that pained his sensitive little nostrils. His mother, whom he had learned to adore and obey in the few short hours of their association, seemed nervous and much concerned. Off in the distance was a dull roar, which, though Bobbie did not know it, told of the oncoming of wildlife's worst enemy—the forest fire.

Momentarily the stifling breath of the fire became thicker. Great clouds of smoke rose high, dipped, and whirled through the forest on agitated air currents. Consternation swept the forest folk: squirrels scampered up trees, chattering their fear; partridges ran aimlessly through the underbrush; wolves and coyotes raced in panic; deer circled in confusion.

Bobbie cried a little in fear. He had expected greater peace in the world than this. His mother was now plainly alarmed. She urged him to his feet and led him away. He stumbled after her, but the travel was difficult, the smoke becoming so thick he could hardly breathe or even see. Frantically his mother drove him on. She ran ahead to hurry him, stamping, snorting, her white tail held high and waving like a flag so he could see her.

The roar came closer, the smoke thickened. Bobbie lost sight of his mother, though he could hear her cry. The direction of the sound led him down toward a valley. He tried hard to go to her, but his little legs were tiring. She came back to him, circled him, and pressed him on, ever guiding him deeper into the lowland. He felt his unsteady feet touch the cool, wet moss of a swamp. Still his mother called him. The great roar seemed all about them, the air so thick Bobbie could no longer breathe, and the crashes of falling trees drowned the guiding voice of his mother.

In panic Bobbie ran aimlessly, bumping into trees and falling over logs. The hungry red flames of the fire were visible now, but, while they burned the trees overhead, they made no progress in the wet moss. Choked, exhausted, his senses swam. He dropped to the ground, overcome.

When Bobbie again opened his eyes, he looked on a different world. There was no smoke to torment his nostrils and no alarming roar. A circle of anxious human faces looked down upon him, and there were little exclamations of delight when he showed signs of life. It was a better world than he had seen before, more like the one he had anticipated. His mother was not there, and this at first gave him a deep feeling of loneliness. But his human benefactors soon showed him that they would meet his needs in food, love, and companionship. Perhaps that mother whose only earthly act was to guide him to safety was some beautiful dream, and these kind people were his real "family."

There were five in this newly adopted family: a sweet mother, whose word he soon learned was law; a tall manly father, who had rescued him from the smoldering ruins of the forest; two sweet little girls, Jean and Beth; and a kindly boy, Howard. The latter three, he quickly found, were to be his playmates; the older folk went about wasting their time at household duties or working in a store when they might be out in the woods.

Though he did not approve of some of their ways of living, Bobbie came to love his family very much. At first they fed him from a bottle, but soon he outgrew this and drank from a pan. And although he required four to six quarts of milk daily, the family gladly supplied the quantity. Later he took to browsing and grazing as a deer should.

At his new home Bobbie never wanted for animal companions. There was a big police dog and, as soon as his legs were strong enough, he took pleasure in showing that dog how to run. They became fast friends and had many a romp together. Then, too, some of his forest relatives learned his whereabouts and called on him.

He was never confined and often went great distances into the forest. During hunting season his family sewed a red-flannel coat on him—a silly thing for them to do, but he loved them so much he would permit them to do anything. However, he did observe that when wearing his red-flannel coat he suffered no injury, while others of his kind were not so fortunate. It was at this time that the family learned something of his extensive wanderings, for hunters saw him many miles from home.

Though he loved his relatives of the wildwood, Bobbie never failed to come at the call of his family, if within hearing distance. Of all sounds, their call was most appealing; of all companions, they were the most desirable. Particularly was he enamored of Jean and Beth, and when they came outdoors to play, he would frisk about like a happy puppy.

One of the family habits, of which he highly approved, was the daily walk. Though this did not always occur at the same time, seldom did the family start down the road but he came bounding out of the woods to ac-

Even the timid fox, famed
for his wild, aloof spirit,
responds to the touch
of friendliness. Wherever
the miracle of life is found,
there likewise lies the capacity
to love and be loved,
placing within our reach
the harmony of heaven.

company them. They were very foolish, he found, holding to roads and beaten trails, and often he tried to coax them deeper into the forest, through swamps and thickets, to the lakes and streams he had found. They did not respond to his proffered guidance, however, and he at last became content to run ahead, to the left and to the right, stealing upon them from behind, and generally demonstrating his superior woodcraft.

Bobbie rather approved of the human custom of living in a house. Of course, it could be greatly overdone, and he thought the family often carried it to extremes; but it wasn't a bad idea at all to get inside where they could all be together—so long as one could get out again!

Once inside he had considerable liberty. Yet there were some things which were not allowed, but why, he could not understand. For instance, it was perfectly all right for him to curl up on a rug and take a nap, but when he got on a bed, the way the rest of the family did, he got spanked. This seemed strange, for it was a much nicer place to sleep. However, the spankings were not very severe, and occasionally he would sneak a few moments on the soft bed, knowing perfectly well what would be the penalty—and not caring either.

The children's nursery was particularly appealing to Bobbie. There were two beds in which his beloved Jean and Beth slept, and a nice soft rug between the beds, which he adopted as his own. This was really his favorite place, and almost every evening he would curl up there until the family was ready to retire. Then it was customary for him to be put out. At times he was so reluctant to go, the mother and father allowed him to stay. On such occasions, at exactly ten minutes of two in the early morning he would come to their bedroom door and ask to be let out. The punctuality of this oft repeated act puzzled the family. Bobbie was sorry he had no way to tell them how he knew the time and how he knew that his companions of the wildwood were then waiting for him. Humans are so stupid, depending on old clocks and things.

One day Bobbie had quite a shock. In the early morning he returned from a hike in the woods, called at the door, and gained admittance. There in the parlor were four of his family: the mother, father, Howard, and Jean. Puzzled, he went into the nursery, but the beds were empty. He came out whining, looked in the corners, then stood gazing into the eyes of one or another of the family, asking his question with all his heart. No one seemed to understand him. He whined and cried until they were almost impatient with him. Then an idea came to the mother. Without saying a word to him, she slipped over and opened the door to another bedroom in which Beth had slept the previous night. With definite purpose he headed straight through the door and found his sleeping playmate. After that he came out and lay down, at peace with the world—all his loved ones accounted for.

Summertime came and Bobbie's spots started to disappear, his coat becoming a beautiful red-brown. His family planned a camping trip to a lake deep in the woods. Bobbie could not be left behind, of course, and neither could the police dog. So the five human beings, the deer, and the dog were packed in a car and went camping.

As at home Bobbie was free to roam the woods about camp, but he showed not the slightest desire to leave. He played on the sands, went swimming, took hikes, and did whatever the family did. Yet he never could quite understand why, if he took part in their habits, they did not join him in his. They didn't seem to care at all about the lovely swamp he had found, they wouldn't run and jump over logs, they wouldn't eat lily pads, and they wasted lovely summer nights sleeping! Oh, well, he couldn't expect them to be perfect. They were lovable just the same.

Winter came on, and with it new joys for Bobbie. His coat turned a dull gray and thickened to meet the low temperatures of the north. He frolicked in the snow and was so happy to find that his Howard, Jean, and Beth loved the snow too. They had great times tumbling and racing about in the beautiful white drifts.

The house became even dearer to him at this season. How he loved the gatherings about the fireplace when all his cherished family was in one spot and he could nudge each one with his nose to let him know he cared. He came to know everything they said to him, and they came to understand his manner of expression too—which shows humans are not so stupid after all.

One day in spring, just a year from the time he was found in the smoking woods, Bobbie waited long for the family to take the afternoon walk. They were busy that day and let some foolish thing like work hinder them from going, so Bobbie went alone. His tracks showed his walk took him in the direction of some people who thought all animals were created just to kill and eat. Bobbie never returned. While it is not known definitely what happened to him, he is not the first deer that ventured near these people and was never seen again.

Bobbie did not live in vain. The story of his sweet companionship and high intelligence has spread far and wide, causing many to have a better understanding of his kind. And deep in the hearts of his family the memory of Bobbie always will be treasured as one of the sweetest gifts of life.

One can scarcely look upon
the spectacle of dawn objectively.
The muted saffron rays that dispel
the dark-velvet shades of night,
calling the world to joy and growth,
clearly symbolize the coming
of awe-inspiring revelation
to human consciousness.

DAWN

Have you ever caught the spirit of the dawn? One may not, legitimately, call himself a true nature lover until he has done so. Perhaps in the freedom of imagination and under guidance of a hundred memories, we may even now reconstruct that ethereal experience.

It will call for all our skill as huntsmen. Many there are who have gone on this mission and come back with gamebags empty. For, if anything alters to the slightest degree our alertness, our lively interest, our sensitiveness to the mystery of the forest, our task is then hopeless. This spirit of the dawn will seize upon any dull moment to slip through our fingers and be gone.

Let us step into the night, feeling that we have left the world of matter behind and found entry into a realm where dreams are true. When fear is absent, the woodland trail at night bristles with beautiful mystery. One feels that everywhere eyes of curious but harmless creatures are staring through the darkness at him—a conviction which, with certain limitations, is probably most often true.

It adds zest to the experience to know that somewhere in the tangled foliage overhead an owl is looking down quizzically at the invaders of night; that rabbits nestle close to the ground and await our passing; that possibly the most clever of creatures, the wildcat, slinks noiselessly behind a bush and watches us with nervous but discerning eyes; that deer may be silently turning their trumpetlike ears toward us to learn more than their eyes can tell; that a wily fox, silent as night itself, glides into his hollow-log retreat and then peeks out cautiously to make sure we pass along.

This drama goes on in the black vastness that engulfs the night traveler in the woods, its charm more deep and effective because the actors are invisible.

As evidence that this is not all fancy, here and there along the route we come overclose to a forest creature who, with startled cry or move, tells us of his presence. We disturb an old ringed-tail coon and catch him in the rays of our flashlight as he scampers over fallen logs and climbs into the darkness. From the top of a little ridge we hear the whistling snort of a deer as the dainty creature tells us in the only way he can his opinion that we do not belong here. A hoot owl lends his voice to the night, sounding as though darkness had spoken— but we resist the temptation to investigate him. We keep steadily on. We must reach the crest of the Great Hill while yet darkness hides our coming.

Are we deep enough into the mood of solitude as yet? Let us pause for a moment and listen. Voices of the ages are speaking. Hear the chorus of frogs, singing a song which was heard when the world was young, which smote the ears of dinosaur and flying reptile. Hear the monotone of insects and the rustle of aspen leaves stirred to dancing by the slightest breeze. Note the mystery of the night bird's call and catch the feel of measureless, dark distance stretching forth from you in every direction. Drink it in, until it becomes a part of you and you a part of it. Let no fragment of the universe escape—take the very stars in your love. Feel that all that has ever been must combine with all that will ever be in making this moment sublime!

We move onward through the darkness, crossing a little creek which murmurs a sweet message to the listening night. And then we climb upward on the fern-covered side of the Great Hill. We reach the crest and look out on the ocean of night below. In the distance is a lake, looking like a great mirror of polished black marble, in which the infinite heavens live again.

Silently we seat ourselves and await an event which has stirred the thoughts of living things since time began. We look toward the east, where the Pleiades are beginning their climb to the zenith. Even as we watch, a pale-gray light dims low-hanging stars and faintly backlights the trees at the horizon. The great moment is at hand and we enter a deeper silence. We tremble with excitement! Our thought is selfless, universal. We cease believing ourselves to be little units of walking matter, but rather eternal witnesses to the ever unfolding glory of creation.

The gray light becomes more intense, and stars scurry in hasty retreat. The world takes form. Shadows slowly vanish. Here is drama that belittles efforts of man. Here is an event that even eternal hills cannot look upon stoically. Our thoughts are lifted up in ecstasy—we have caught the spirit of the dawn!

There, in the distance, is the first birdcall, a robin who feels the resurrecting touch. Another answers him. Reaching everywhere at once, the dawn awakens all the musicians of the forest. White-throated sparrows, olive-backed thrushes, vireos, linnets, warblers of every description, song sparrows, red-winged blackbirds, chickadees, juncos—all raise voice to the dawn, and even the harsh calls of raven and crow sound rich in this setting. Now see how the dawn awakens the trees and causes wild flowers to lift their dew-covered heads. It crowns hilltops with gold, and the heavens blush at its caress.

A sacred duty rests with the dawn: to see that the sun hears in nature nothing but song and looks on nothing but beauty. Though we have caught the spirit of the dawn and have it locked within our hearts, yet it cannot be limited and confined. Forever and ever it goes before the sunlight, calling nature from slumber and drawing song from all living things. In our thoughts we trail it about the globe as through unfailing magic it enlivens the world, tints the ocean swell, gilds the rock-bound island, awakens palm and pine, finding life forever young and beautiful.

Now day brightens! Our hearts have had their fill of beauty, and we make our way back to the lodge where we may think upon the loveliness we have seen and strive to keep alive in our breasts the captured spirit of the dawn. But pause a moment. Is there not a symbol in what we have seen and felt? Is there not a mental dawn fast trailing the night of human experience? And is there not a spirit—hope, faith, inspiration—which sets the heart to singing and prepares it for the full understanding?

His song blends perfectly with all that is good and beautiful. Is it sound or the rush of exalted thought?

VOICES OF BIRDS

A CARDINAL filled the wintry air with his cheery song. It was pleasant to hear, for even beyond the beauty of the music itself was the fact that he had risen above the notion that winter is a bleak season, devoid of warm joy and happiness.

Certainly the cardinal song is a happy one. In quality of tone he mimics the jolly laughter of a happy winter sportsman. He has all the glee of the tobogganist, the joyous shouts of skaters, and the song of sleigh parties, ski and snowshoe enthusiasts. His voice shows he has discovered that true spring is in the heart, not in the season or a landscape. He sings not because the world is filled with song, but because he is. He is the philosopher of birdland, speaking plainly and clearly his conviction that life is what one makes it and that the outside world only mirrors one's own thoughts. His voice has the tone of confidence. He knows whereof he speaks. There is a positiveness in his musical assertions that shakes the fortitude of the most profound pessimist. Yet his style is not argumentative, merely a simple statement of indisputable fact.

God bless him!—the songster of the snows. How noble he looks sitting on a barren bough, his brilliant plumage a startling contrast to the white beauty of the winter day, his song a reprimand to every dull, doubting, or discouraging thought.

A robin sang in the soft, sacred silence of that mysterious hour when night rides the tresses of closing day. It was the clear-cut song of one who, with neither guile nor conceit, sings in confidence of his own sincerity. There was a neighborliness in his tone.

The robin's voice is not that of the social lion, the one superior or apart. He is the friend to whom one talks with abandon, passes the time of day, jokes with courageous familiarity, with whom first names are sufficient. He sings in a beautiful vernacular, and we love him for his sweet approachableness. His voice is the kind we would hear in our parlor, over the dinner table, or at a community picnic. He speaks the language of friend, neighbor, or family.

A thousand blessings on the robin, as through song he reminds all of the beauty of everyday things and people, sets us to being grateful for the miracle of every hour, and awakens anew the realization that nowhere in the universe will we find creation of greater moment than that which touches us on every side.

The wild bergamot grows in regions
where meadowlarks like to nest,
and it poses a visible echo
to their lovely, melodious songs.
Theirs is the natural kinship
between birds and flowers,
and they are forever helping
each other in matters
of food and propagation.

A white-throated sparrow sang forth from behind the delicate drapes of darkness. His song echoed among the stars. Then he began it again. He held long to one plaintive note and ended with the strain incomplete, as though he could recall no more of it.

His is the voice and the manner of mystery. One cannot tell from whence his singing comes, or indeed if it is not the voice of night itself. He speaks the language of the dreamer who has glimpsed a higher truth. He lives, thinks, and sings in poetry—being "in the world but not of it." The silver tones he breathes into solitude drip with mysticism. He chants the truth of the unbelievable; and in the magic of his voice the forest becomes peopled with fairies and sprites of heavenly order. There is no fear, and nothing fearsome, in the song of the whitethroat, even though it is ever in the realm of the unseen.

Immeasurable gratitude to and for the white-throated sparrow. His gossamer song shames all that is gross, coarse, crude, and vulgar and speaks not of a better world than this, but of a better view of the one in which we live.

The wood thrush greeted the dawn with a song unmatched in musical quality by any other feathered songster. The clear, dual, bell-like tones echoed through the forest chambers, adding a luster to retreating shadows.

Here is the voice of a whole-souled lover of the world, which garnishes with loveliness everything within its range. It is the voice of the true minister, the unreserved public benefactor who "loves all men, but none too much." It has the rich resonance we expect in one who has within his heart no smallness, no trickery, no selfishness. It is the courageous confidence of bold faith. It has the quality which, when found among men, causes all other voices to be silent when it speaks and precludes argument and opposition by its very strong assurance. In the human singer the quality of the wood thrush makes listeners feel that the artist is one of them—close, friendly, confidential; in the orator the same quality draws hearers so near to the speaker's side that only his convictions seem to exist; in the conversationalist it creates such charm that all wish to remain silent to give him who has it more opportunity to speak.

Joy and infinite life to that wood thrush, and may the rich resonance of his voice be present in all worlds that are or may be, adding beauty to beauty, serenity to solitude, tranquillity to forest depths, and heavenly peace to the wilderness atmosphere.

Raindrops filter
through the umbrella of foliage,
cleansing and refreshing
the mass of vegetation.
A drop is a tiny thing,
but it holds the secret of growth
and is the seed of earth's
numberless lakes and streams.

RAIN

THERE is much beauty about rain, both to hear and to see. I love to watch it as it sifts through the needles of evergreen trees or drives in sheets across an open lake.

Rain always seems to be having such a good time. It is never aloof, never self-righteous, never flaunting a "holier-than-thou" attitude, but falls alike "on the just and unjust." Joyfully it descends to earth, giving its nourishing goodness to all living things, not stopping to call one plant "weed," another "flower." It rides the wind through the forest, cleansing the air which carries it, bathing and refreshing the face of the earth, and finally, in tiny rivulets of its own creation, sings its way into lake, stream, and sea.

And I love to hear the song of rain on the cabin roof. Some poets have referred to this as the "patter," but that word is inadequate. Others call it a "drone," but that too seems poor description. Rain on the roof does not give a note that is musicless, nor does it play a monotone. At first attention it may seem so, but if you listen more closely, you will know that there is a constant fluctuation of pitch, which grows into a soft melody. Rain does not patter on the roof, it sings on the roof—Mother Nature's own cradle song.

The forest is always so grateful for rain. Trees come out dripping, flushed with new life, as a boy who has taken a hasty swim. Moss and grass sparkle with fresh beauty, and lovely flowers, bowing heads in prayers of thanksgiving, blush deeper hues at the blessings showered upon them.

Sad experiences are teaching us how little we understand rain. We have thought its only cycle was to rise from the sea, fall to the earth, and flow back to its nativity. It has taken floods and droughts to awaken the realization that in nature's scheme rain does not fall evenly throughout the year, and that the surplus of one season must be retained for the lack of the next.

The undisturbed landscape of nature is much like a sponge, soaking up the water which falls upon it. Every growing thing has its part in this play. It is calculated that a virgin forest will retain all but 15 per cent of a rainfall, whereas a treeless area will lose 60 per cent, and a plowed region 80 per cent at once. Every beaver pond, swamp, and lake is a part of the storage system for this life-giving rain water.

It is easy to see what sad folly it has been for the human race to trap out so many beavers, blast their dams, drain swamps, cut forests mercilessly. Small wonder that waters, which would be retained by the intricate storage system, race down the rivers, leaving a path of destruction in their wake.

In the Midwest there is a river on which I often camped when a boy. Until a few years ago the territory about its source and headwaters was a nature lover's paradise. The river arose in a wide network of bayous, totaling several miles in width. This area was timber covered, a haven for small game and birds, its waters alive with fish. Then ambitious and unwise businessmen drained it by running a dredge ditch right through the center. They argued that the river-bottom land would be ideal for farming and carried their plan through under the pretense of public benefaction. The river was ruined and *the land reclaimed proved to be worthless.* Now only empty farm buildings can be seen in the area, and each spring the river races down its artificial course in varying flood stages.

It is probable that we are somewhat in error when we insist so determinedly that trees are the source of much rain. It is true that each tree releases enormous quantities of water into the air daily, and that it is condensation of moisture that we call rain. But trees could not give off water which had not first been given them. It is rain which is responsible for the presence of trees, not trees which create rain. The function of the forest is to retain and slowly distribute the rain received. Growth rings of trees which have been on earth thousands of years show that there have always been

53

fluctuations of water fall. Periods of small rainfall were experienced before man's atrocious destruction of the forest. But trees and swamps were then present to tide over these periods by holding parsimoniously the treasure heaven had entrusted to them.

Like our banks, which do not create money but store it, the grand purpose of the forest with its many tiny and great storage vaults is to hold the liquid gold of nature and proportion its circulation. And only as we restore swamp conditions and beaver flowages in our river headwaters, plant again the forests and guard their growth, can we re-establish that link in the circulation of the earth's rainfall, without which the world is in a sad way.

A sage has said, "Man marks the earth with ruin." Everywhere we see scars of our folly. Nor can we say that what our race did yesterday was foolish, but today we are wise. There seems to be only one wisdom and that is to interfere as little as possible with the natural order of things.

It is far better for us if we adapt ourselves to nature as we find it rather than vainly attempt to change nature to fit our ideas. Fundamental laws are unalterable. They are part of a perfect wisdom which is quite different from that which we call, questionably, the "wisdom of men." For brief periods we seem to make improvements on nature, altering her habits and appropriating her laws. But before long a reaction occurs, and all our triumphs are revealed as but illusions.

Have you ever stood in a virgin forest where the law and order of nature are best revealed? There is a sense of eternity that comes to one's thought. The air is cool and moist as the great trees give forth invisible but enormous quantities of the rain entrusted to their care. Lakes and streams look more at home here than they do in a disturbed area. There is a feeling of perfect balance. And to me there comes this realization: if man would allow these universal laws—natural to the world and to him—to operate without interference, he would more quickly become conscious of the perfect state of being for which he yearns.

For I am sure that beauty, power, balance, evenness are truly fundamental in nature. And I am equally sure that brotherly love, service, and Christianly principles are basic with man. Human inventions inject all disturbances into both nature and man. "God hath made man upright; but they have sought out many inventions."

The worth of rain is never more obvious than when one steps out into a forest just after a storm. How fresh and lovely everything is! The air seems to cleanse one within as he breathes it. Birds sing with new brilliance. It is as though the skies had showered a bit of heaven upon earth, a blessing which, in the natural order of things, would remain long sufficient unto the needs of the day.

The river is a master minstrel,
and endless is the tale it tells.
Its muted, lulling tones lead us
to the margin of dreamland
where the nice distinction
between fact and fairytale
is difficult to discern—
and we experience the dramas
its waters relate.

❧ A RIVER IS BORN

THE moment finds us at the birthplace of a river. A pool before us marks the place where many springs bubble forth clear, cold water—water which pauses for a moment as though to gain sense of direction, and then starts off for the sea.

What a long, winding course is before these waters. Yet they will sing their way under, over, through, or around all obstacles until they are home again. For water knows no home but the sea, and it is ever restless until it reaches there.

Wouldn't you like to follow these waters on their journey? What beautiful things must lie along their course, what happy experiences they must encounter. Here, in the pool that marks their first view of the world, they pause in deliberate calmness to contemplate the heavens and mirror back the beauty which shines upon them. In a playful whirlpool they circle about as if toying with the beautifully marked trout to which they offer hospitality. Then strumming a marching song on streamside rocks, reeds, willows, and fallen logs, they begin their long, difficult journey without fear.

The waters mingle patience with courage, moving slowly through deep channels or pitching over sudden waterfalls with unimpeachable poise. They will play with the pebbles which roll down their course, subtly undermine great boulders, clamber clumsily over fallen logs, or slyly creep beneath them, never weary, never bored, never faultfinding, and never sad. Back in the deep recesses of the forest they will hold rendezvous with many shy wilderness creatures. Lovely deer will drink of their refreshing liquid; lumbering bears will wade their shallows and cubs play in their rapids; birds will bathe in their still pools; and feverish creatures, wounded by the thoughtless and cruel acts of men, will creep to the streamside seeking sympathy and relief. The waters will seep back through the banks of the stream, sort out the roots of plants and trees, and nourish these to new growth. They will mellow the hot winds of summer or sing on under the blanket of winter—nothing can stop them, for they are going home, going to the sea.

I love rivers. They seem symbolic of life eternal, for they never cease to be. A lake is only a river waiting to go somewhere. Some day its waters must break from their rest and seek the sea. A river is that seeking—and that seeking is forever.

I have found rivers in very odd places indeed. In the Blue Ridge Mountains of Virginia I came upon a tiny river emerging into the world from a mountainside. It seemed as if it were stealing in, for it came from behind a rock and divided its course as if in attempt to escape detection. It ran down the slope quickly to join other waters, seeking obscurity in the masses.

In Mammoth Cave, Kentucky, I climbed down 360 feet below the surface of the ground and there found a large-sized river flowing along rapidly over a route that was dark, weird, and difficult. Yet these waters sang just as happily as do the sun-kissed mountain streams, and when they entered a great cavern, they raised their voices as if enjoying their own echoes.

In the desert region of the west is a stream that flows along the surface of the ground for some distance and then, apparently tiring of the desert heat, disappears into the earth. For miles there is no trace of it, but ultimately it comes once more into daylight, much cooled and energized by its experience. At Silver Springs, Florida, a gigantic river suddenly comes up from the earth, so great in volume that large boats may float over its very source.

I love rivers. It was a river that first drew back the curtains and let me look upon a poetic phase of nature. It introduced me to a phenomenon which has stayed with me ever since, never losing any of the charm and mystery which attended the first experience. When a boy, I camped near the source of this one river. Its waters move very rapidly; they are fed into one central channel from a number of small tributaries Its ragged streamsides are covered with brush, and many are the logs, shrubs, and stones which reach out into the passing waters to strum melodies.

On the first night I camped in this region, I was quite wakeful. Everything is always so interesting and exciting the first night in camp that I have no desire then to slumber. My companions were more drowsy than I, however, and soon I was the only one in camp not asleep. I lay there listening to the many sounds of the night and woods.

Suddenly I heard human voices! The sound seemed to originate just beyond the bend of the river. I quickly concluded it was another group of campers who had neglected to make camp early enough. From the sound of their voices, they seemed happy, good-humored people, and I hurriedly dressed, thinking I could help them find a site. I went out of the tent and lighted a lantern; there was no one in sight on the river. I waved the lantern as a signal, but there was no response. And I could no longer hear the voices.

Puzzled, I went back to bed again, but now sleep was impossible. After some minutes my thoughts quieted, and I heard the songs of crickets and tree toads. Then before I realized it, I was listening to the voices of that camping party again. I could hear high-pitched laughter and almost make out words. Whoever they were, they seemed to be having such a wonderful time that I hoped they would camp near us. I lighted the lantern again, and this time I walked down to the edge

A waterfall, be it large or small, forever impresses man
with the beauty, power, and permanence of nature.

of the racing waters and swung my light from side to side. But as before, there was no response, and then I lost the sound. I was tempted to call my companions, but did not.

A score of suggestions came to my perplexed mind, yet none of them satisfactory. I stood for some time looking into the night, and although once or twice I thought I heard a voice, it was impossible to be sure. Now becoming a bit weary, for most of the night was gone, I returned to the tent and to bed. When about half asleep, the sound of voices came once more, but this time I dismissed them with the thought that if there was a party needing aid, they would see our camp.

The next day I spoke to one more versed in wood-craft than I. It was then I learned of one of the most mysterious things in nature, the "voices of the woods." Woods people are familiar with them. In the deep quiet of night in the forest and particularly near fast moving streams, these voices come. They always sound like happy, carefree travelers.

Unquestionably one is but hearing the sound of singing waters and other woodland sounds, all rolled into one. Our ears interpret this effect in light of our human experience, and we believe we hear human voices. If one keeps fear and superstition from spoiling his happiness, the voices of the woods are beautiful, the experience of hearing them inspiring. I have heard them since in many parts of the wilderness, yet I always feel deeply grateful to the river which first introduced them to me.

I love rivers—and while it is said that one should never love anything that is lifeless, I believe I am not violating this rule. Rivers are living ideas. They are functional parts of a living universe. They are, as the veins and arteries of nature, a part of the life of all living things. I love them from source to sea and over the invisible route which brings them back to source again.

The antlered buck is a soul-stirring sight, as essential to wilderness charm as trees are to the forest.

THE ANTLERED KING

MIDNIGHT in woodland wilderness!

A full moon dominates the sky, bathing the north country in cool splendor. A mood of perfect calm holds the elements. All at the Sanctuary are wrapped in peaceful sleep; all save two—two canoeists. They skirt the lake shores, slipping noiselessly through long, black shadows cast by shore-line trees. They emerge at the small clearing which marks the deer run.

"He's there!" whispers one, his voice startling him.

"Stroke!" answers the other.

One! Two! Three! Three sharp strokes and the canoe is left to momentum, the while the paddlers sit motionless. So smooth is the run of the light craft it seems suspended in space while the universe glides by.

"He's feeding," whispers one.

The other commands silence, perhaps not too politely, and steers the drifting canoe toward a ghostly form at the water's edge.

Standing like the incarnate "spirit of the wilderness" is the most noble of bucks, known to us all as the antlered king. A glimpse of him is a trophy prized at the Sanctuary. He has been sighted on the Spruce Swamp Trail, twice at Vanishing Lake, and his great tracks have been the outstanding discovery of several hikes. This morning the sands at this spot bore record of a nocturnal visit, and the canoeists have gambled a few hours' sleep on the theory that he might return.

They have guessed well, and rich is their reward. There he stands—a king indeed. In the mystic moonlight he seems more the specter of some vanquished monarch of the forest, come to haunt his former domain. His antlered head is held proudly aloft as he munches delectable lily pads. Now, as he reaches down for another bite, the canoeists take a quick stroke in his direction and then sit motionless as he looks up again.

Several more well-timed strokes and they are but fifty feet away. The momentum carries them to forty—to thirty—to twenty-five! Then they drift to twenty—twenty feet from the antlered king. Here is adventure! He stands still now, suspicious of the floating shadow, an offshore draft denying him the testimony of his nostrils. The canoeists scarcely breathe; and they fear lest the loud beating of their hearts betray them. But they are safe so long as there is no sudden motion, no noise, and the forest breeze keeps their scent from him; for the human scent is alarm to all beasts of the woods— shame be to man!

Little creatures like the borer deepen nocturnal solitude
and add exotic aura to the drama of darkness.

The king stands erect, his ears forward—the picture of wilderness caution. He seems like some angelic dream that will dissolve at the slightest disturbance. Never, never will the canoeists forget these few moments—perhaps ten, perhaps thirty, they cannot tell. The beautiful creature scarcely four paddle lengths before them, the birches at the shore line no less ethereal than he, the dark mass of the forest, and *silence*—silence that is engraving the scene in the core of their hearts!

The king becomes reconciled to the presence of the shadow: a misplaced cloud, no doubt, crowded from the sky by the moonlight. He returns to his meal. Every motion sings with grace and rhythm—the delicate bowing of his neck, the dainty pawing of his slender hoofs, and the occasional tossing of his head as if to wave proudly his magnificent antlers before an admiring world. The canoeists sit entranced, drinking in every sound and filmy object of the exquisite scene. A fish flops some distance away, knowing just when this sound should enter the silent symphony, and on the far shore the cry of an owl is heard at decorous intervals.

Quietly and unnoticed another spectator watches this sylvan drama. An old beaver, rich in forest wisdom, swims noiselessly in the deeper waters. He is curious about the principals in this nocturnal scene. The antlered king he has seen often before, and of him feels no fear. But that strange floating log, with figures at either end, excites both his curiosity and suspicion. Still unnoticed he moves very slowly toward the object. It is so still it puzzles him. His nose nearly touches it when suddenly he gains the terrifying scent of man! It is the scent he has often encountered when death thundered among his people; the scent borne likewise by the atrocious steel traps that torture his kind. As a warning to all wild creatures, he strikes the water a resounding smack with his great flat tail and dives to safety.

The canoeists, still under the spell of woodland wilderness, are unprepared for this sharp noise of gunshot proportions at the very side of their canoe. They spring upright, the canoe lurching and tipping menacingly. There is a clatter of falling flashlights and paddles —a bursting of noise that animates the scene.

Up goes the antlered head, the flaglike tail, and the king is gone! Oh, the sublime grace of that flight: great leaps made without seeming effort; a bold dash back into the dark woodland; and then only the sound of hoofs, crackling twigs, and resentful whistling snorts mark his route through the forest until he is swallowed up in silence. Out in the open lake the old beaver, proud of the disturbance he has caused, continues his smacking and diving.

The canoeists paddle slowly back to the Sanctuary, still under the spell of the adventure. They beach the canoe before either speaks and then, "Man, what we have to tell them in the morning!"

The mellow, silver light
of the moon has a quality
quite different from the sun.
It deepens distances,
enshrouds the forest aisles
with mystery, inspires
the weird calls of owl and loon,
and reveals a phase of beauty
otherwise unseen by man.

THE PROMISE
OF THE CRESCENT MOON

THE crescent moon sailed in the western sky, in the gathering shades of evening a dainty sliver of light so faint it might easily have been overlooked. But it was there, and it gained in strength as daylight faded. It crept through the tops of pine trees as all other moons had done before it, found its way to the horizon where it seemed to pause for a moment, reluctant as a child who must go to bed—and there in its rich, young beauty it showed for a moment its promise. Outlined by what appeared to be a dark light, yet wholly distinct, were its greater portions, nine-tenths of its glorious self which only the future could reveal.

In its loveliness, suspended among the stars, floating on the omnipotent laws of creation, it said anew that nothing that is good and beautiful can ever be lost to the universe. In a voice that made no sound, it promised to glow with all the glory shown by all moons that had gone before it. It would grow with the days and ways

71

of the universe. It would bathe silent landscapes with mystic light. It would caress shy creatures as they moved from shadow to shadow, and wing the song of the whip-poorwill.

Nightly its shining surface would enlarge and enlarge, increasing the power of its influence, until it would reach the fullness of its glory. It would rise upon the eastern horizon just as the sun sank in the west, as if to challenge the very supremacy of the king of the skies. It would rise majestically aloft, a great silver disk, so brilliant that only the greatest of stars dared brave its presence. It would stir hearts and minds as deeply as had its progenitors, and though one had lived to see a thousand moons, he would say of this, "It is the loveliest of all."

Crescent Moon, we love your promise. You write truth in the heavens. By the miracle of your being, you turn our thoughts from decay and despair to startling and joyous realization of the eternal youthfulness of the universe. Wisdom points out in you the parable which teaches that youth is not a fleeting stage of growth soon to be swallowed up in decay—it is a principle of nature. Youth shall forever appear on the horizon of creation— the freshness of young things shall never cease to be.

Now we see your lesson more widely in nature, O Crescent Moon! While the great white pine lets its head droop and its branches slowly become barren, we note the buoyant green of the ambitious little tree at its roots. While a billion trees, fallen to the ground in senseless

Baby owls enter the world prepared for a masquerade.
To think that such a face is really their own!

waste, make soil of themselves, a billion more, crowned with the vibrant joy of youth, rise to say forests shall not perish from the earth. There is the thin, unsteady voice of the nestling, which gives promise that all skies of the future shall echo with bird songs as sweet as have ever been sung. Here is the mighty mountain range, hoary with age, worn with the rains and winds of time— yet the very earth beneath it creeps and groans as new ranges, youthful ranges likely to rise higher than any known before, are being born.

Yes, youth is ingrained in the universe. It joins hands with the steadiness of maturity and wisdom of age, as an eternal completeness. To this truth we may fasten our faith. Life will never cease to sparkle with newness, freshness, youngness, nor will it lose the rich treasures of experience.

In the promise of the crescent moon we see our tragedies and fears belittled. The blustering conqueror will sink into oblivion, his boasted deeds and bloated powers fade with the dream in which they were made— the universe of reality will flow on. The shriek of shell and roar of cannon will draw back their echoes, and silence reign. Birds will perch upon rusted guns and sing —sing in youthful, happy voices, as glorious as ever before known. Flowers will grow in unused trenches, trees seed themselves in the crumbled dust of thrones, mushrooms crack gun emplacements—the youth of the world will be manifest! Babes will come into the world bringing fresh revelations of age-old truths. They will look beautiful, though slight and delicate, on life's horizon. Yet they will bear a precious power and promise. They will belie the fearful prediction that goodness may be lost to the human race. They will have within themselves that glory natural to creation. They will have all the shining beauty and brilliance seen in the finest of the generations before them, and they will have the power and purpose to carry civilization to greater heights than ever before.

Civilization shall not perish from the face of the earth. The heavenly order of things will not permit it. "Behold, I make all things new!"—the Creator forever makes them new. The youth are not youthful by choice, but by this principle upon which the universe is founded. This principle, forever manifesting itself, forever pouring its very nature into the world—this the immortal substance of youth is the prophetic hope of the world. Such is the promise of the crescent moon.

The calls of frogs and toads
are among the oldest vocal sounds.
They arose from ancient pools
and echoed through primeval jungles.
No other voice speaks so plainly
of those wild, primitive ages
when the earth was young.

THE MYSTERY
OF THE TWILIGHT HOUR

NATURE'S favorite drama is the mystery thriller. She writes always in the same vein and never finishes a story. Her manuscript is endless, act upon act, but never a finale—never a falling curtain.

Nature reserves her choicest subtleties for certain moods of men. Not everyone is accepted in her inner chambers, not any one at all times. Only through the most complete self-forgetfulness and unreserved surrender to receptive mood are her exotic tenses revealed.

So it is with the mystery of the twilight hour. Have you ever witnessed it? Then come with me, but I suggest you leave all surplus weight behind. No, I do not refer to your coats and wraps; the chill air of evening will be upon us early, and you will need them. But you will have no need for burdening thoughts gathered in the world of men. If you have brought with you ill will for any living being—leave it behind. Or if resentment, injured pride, jealousy, or revenge are with you—drop them now.

These are the real burdens that will handicap you and keep your thought from climbing to the heights of full beauty and life.

In the fading light of day we follow a deer runway along the edge of a great swamp. The runway is worn deep in the soil, having been used for uncounted years by these lovely creatures. It is carpeted with moss and outlined by sweet fern. Trailing arbutus looks up at us in sweet humility and whispers a greeting in perfumed breath. We pass between venturesome tamarack trees— trees that have dared leave the multitudes of the swamp and climb boldly to higher ground. (A beautiful tree is the tamarack, its clusters of short, green needles looking much like stars. At that, the tamarack is a bit of a pretender: it looks like an evergreen, and often is mistaken as such, but nevertheless sheds its needles each year as do the broad-leaved trees of the north.)

The sun is low in the west when we come to a great rock, rising like a sentinel out of a verdant sea. We climb it and find its surface scarred by the glacier, its sides worn by the waves of waters long since vanished. We seat ourselves on its high crest and look out over silent, green legions of trees that fill the valley. They suggest a great army of soldiers that might have faced the sly trickery of gods and were magically changed from men to trees as they stood, never to march again. Or is it that they are only marking time until the day is done and back of the curtain of night will spring to life in swift movements that we shall never see, carrying on a purpose we cannot know? Perhaps that murmuring voice of the spring which flows from the nearby hillside even now is giving them orders in a tongue they alone understand.

The sun touches the western horizon and tree shadows lengthen. The cool breath of the forest caresses our cheeks, and leads us to draw our wraps tightly around us. From hidden depths of the swamp arise little curls of vapor. "Indian campfires," legend says, and it is told that the spirits of departed red men return under the veil of dusk to roam their former haunts and gather in councils about fires which never burn.

But another mist is rising, invisible to the eye, yet felt by the very soul. It is the mystery of the twilight hour! The sun has slipped below the horizon, and high gossamer clouds stand out against the steel-blue sky in brilliant pink, like a colorful scarf with which the day is waving farewell. A wedge of ducks in military formation, wings whistling, drive through the still air, as unswerving in their flight as an arrow. A great blue heron, trim and graceful, wings his way across our field of vision, while from the distance comes the harsh, low-pitched call of his cousin, the night heron.

Gently the twilight hour, jealous of its treasures, blindfolds our eyes to all but the budding stars and fading afterglow. Our ears toy with the intriguing sounds of dusk. Frogs and insects chant their lay, and from near or far, high or low—we cannot tell—comes the superlative song of the hermit thrush.

Now let us reach a deeper level of silence within our thoughts. Cease willfully to hear or see, and let yourselves feel the mystery of the twilight hour.

Do you not catch it? A something beyond sound, beyond sight, a measured beat as though you felt the metronome of the universe? How often the nature lover has mentally turned and run when this came to him, directed his thoughts to the study of color or form, or to unraveling the mystery of half-heard sounds. We fear the very fineness of spiritual experiences.

That which we feel is not the black shadows of approaching night, not the twinkle of the stars, nor the fluctuation of the afterglow; it is not depth or distance, not the sound of growing trees, nor yet the footsteps of shadows—though imagination might argue it to be any or all of these. *It is the persistent, pulsing, throbbing rhythm of the wilderness.*

Is it a sound or not? One cannot say. Perhaps woods people hear it with a more acute hearing, or maybe it is only felt. But it is real, tangible, and the whole universe sways to it. I have felt it wherever and whenever the peace of the twilight hour has brought true silence to my thought: in the virgin forests of Canada; in the redwoods of California; in the mountains, deserts, or at the seashore.

Look now upon the tamarack valley fading to blackness. See the last faint rosy blush of the afterglow and the first timid ring of the Aurora in the northern sky. Note the silvery brilliance of the Milky Way as it stretches from horizon to horizon. Catch the murmur of the night wind as it strokes the pines. Now give ear to the multitude of voices that speak forth without marring the silence. From among the leaves and tangled brush along the swamp margin rise the chatter and squeak of little ground creatures. In the distance we hear the howl of a wolf, and comes the shrill trill of a raccoon. Tree toads and crickets are calling. The soft draperies of night are drawn before the ever perceived but never solved mystery of the twilight hour.

Back in the forest depths,
accessible only to the most
untiring nature lover,
lies this lovely, limpid lake,
now vanishing as sphagnum moss
reaches in from its shores.
It is a secret rendezvous
where forest folk may meet
and sylvan sprites hold festival.

5 VANISHING LAKE

THERE were two of us returning over the ancient Indian Trail from Lone Stone Lake to the Sanctuary of Wegimind. The day was closing and we were stepping lively. About midway through, while noting the industry of a brown creeper, we discovered an old blaze high on a Norway pine. Its obvious age and the possible attempt to conceal it by placing it high excited our curiosity. The sap from the tree had long since coated the wound, precluding decay, but had not obscured it. How it had escaped our attention these many months we could not begin to understand.

We stepped beyond the Norway; there were more blazes—a trail! Some arboreal spirit from unsounded depths had ventured forth and returning had only partially concealed his tracks. It was an irresistible invitation to the unexplored depths of the forest, and though the hour was a bit late to follow a blazed trail, we pursued it with boyish abandon.

The blazes were well-made, one on each side of the tree to indicate the direction of travel, and cut beyond the inner bark. They had not been hacked or chipped out, but made with one stroke of a belt-ax—the work of a woodsman, either white or red. Where they led we did not know, but it must be to adventure, for blazed trails are not made promiscuously in the north country.

We stole along as silently as possible, subconsciously trying to imitate the noiseless tread of the fictional Indian, though feeling somewhat as trespassers on an estate of the wilderness gods. The blazes led us through a charming variety of woods: into groves of white pine; over ridges capped with maples and birch; into long, smooth-carpeted aisles of hemlock; and through labyrinths of tamarack and swamp spruce. We were alive with the thrill of discovery and yet impatient to find the trail's objective. The sun did not pause for our convenience, and the twilight in the woods was rapidly obliterating the blazes.

We were in the mood to turn back, with the promise of another visit, when we arrived at the foot of a steep hill. As if testing our nerve, the trail turned uncompromisingly up the steepest part—perhaps to shake itself free of weaklings. In whispered tones (it would have been irreverent to talk aloud in this great silence) we discussed the advisability of going farther; yet our feet, wiser than we, were climbing upward as we talked. Without voicing a decision, we ceased talking to save our breath for the ascent. At points it was so steep we

To hear the silent sermon of the jack-in-the-pulpit, one must kneel humbly among the green congregation.

traveled as much by strength of arm as by leg, using the saplings to draw ourselves upward. Still the blazes led up and on, like a siren leading us to some desired fate.

Then we reached the crest! It was dusk. It was still— so still. We were treading paths few had followed. We were adrift in an infinite forest, a sea of gigantic, virile, yet friendly, trees. We were conscious of the wilderness!

Self-forgetful, in a mood of quivering expectancy, we looked upon a little, unnamed lake of such virginal splendor, we gasped in admiration. It seemed another world, as though we were gazing on the materialization of some poetic fantasy. In the gathering twilight the vast forest became a downy nest, cradling the tiny lake. It was merely a stone's throw across it, though the contour of the country showed plainly that on some geological yesterday the lake had been much larger. But it had been overgenerous with its waters; the sun, the wind, and gravity had taken more from it than they had returned; and now it rested quietly entrenched in the center of its former domain, having lost much of its bulk but none of its beauty. Sphagnum moss was creeping out from its shores—moss that slowly consumes sedentary waters and renders land. It seemed as if Nature had one day here opened her hand to reveal a priceless jewel, and now affectionately was again closing her fist on the treasure. Slowly, silently, gloriously, the lake was *vanishing!*

Fleecy clouds overhead caught the first pink tones of sunset, and the placid waters below mirrored the color back to us. On the farther shore, dim in dusk and distance, we could faintly make out the form of a deer. We felt we were stealing a glimpse into the sanctuary of the forest king.

Should we go on? Should we advance to the shores of these delightful waters? Touch them familiarly? No! No! At least not now. Such charm is like the great minds of mankind: most beautiful at a distance. We would not disturb the atmosphere of awe; we would not break the exotic aura by being overfamiliar. What we had taken thus far would never be missed; but we knew if we greedily grasped for more, we would have less. The spell of thrilling mystery, the primitive beauty, the half-eerie charm of wilderness—all would flee to some remote spot if we pressed them.

We turned silently and made our way back over the trail. Fortunately we reached our own lake and our waiting canoe before darkness rendered the forest an impenetrable wall. We sat late before the glowing fireplace, dreaming much, saying little, but filled with gratitude for the bountiful gifts of the day. Vanishing Lake was added to the vast store of sacred treasures at the Sanctuary of Wegimind.

Drumming, drumming, drumming—
the ruffed grouse beats
his strange rhythm
on muffled tom-toms,
greeting the oncoming dawn.
A chorus of birds' voices
accompanies the drumming,
swelling the prelude.

PRELUDE TO DAWN

AN ORNITHOLOGIST of England, having both intellect and heart aplenty, once conceived the joyful task of charting the bird songs which greet the dawn. What a poetic concept! Dwell upon it for a moment and see to what fine precepts it brings you.

We are likely to think of dawn as it comes to us daily at our peculiar station on the earth. But think of it as a thing in itself—think how it would be if we could travel with the dawn. Eternally creeping, creeping, rolling back a night which it never truly sees, the dawn moves about the earth, steadily, inevitably, without sound or friction. The world animates everywhere at its touch. Trees reach for its life-giving light; winds awaken to motion; man steps forth to meet a new day. And the birds—the birds, from pole to pole along the fringe of the breaking wave of light, symbolic of the Creator's gift of consciousness, take to wing or perch, raising their voices in a massive prelude to dawn. Never are their hearts more full of the joy of living, never their voices sweeter, or their praise clearer, than when the long-curved fingers of the sun reach before its coming and awaken the feathered hordes. What says Longfellow?

> Think every morning when the sun peeps through
> The dim, leaf-latticed windows of the grove,
> How jubilant the happy birds renew
> Their old, melodious madrigals of love!
> And when you think of this, remember too
> 'Tis always morning somewhere, and above
> The awakening continents, from shore to shore,
> Somewhere the birds are singing evermore.

Indeed the choir which greets the dawn is far spread. Man can only speculate on the grandeur of this endless prelude and build in thought wondrous conceptions based upon the small fragment of this drama which lies before him.

Look out into the Sanctuary. In the first gray streaks of dawn, before the stars have deserted the skies, the call comes. The unseen baton of the invisible Maestro waves, and the soft, mystic notes of the whitethroat respond. The wood thrush picks up the strain, running up through the chromatic scale, marvelously dwelling upon his bell-like dual tones at appropriate intervals; now the song sparrow, with his bouncing, happy song, and the robins whose oft repeated melodies never surfeit. At times the notes of the hermit and the veery, the dainty murmuring song of the waxwing, the rhythmic call of the oriole, the soft sweet voices of a multitude of warblers, the "unmusical" calls of the gull, the heron, the loon, and the chatter of the kingfisher—all blend to make the supreme choral effect. And this much of the glorious prelude may be heard on an acre; think what this means when multiplied to include the ends of the earth.

Bring in the nightingale, the famed warblers of the mountains, the southern mockingbirds, the multitudinous birds of the tropics. What magnificence, this musicale supreme! We thrill to the depth of our hearts to hear a portion of it once in twenty-four hours on our small acre; but to the dawn it comes from areas without limit, beginning when life began, and knowing neither pause nor finale as life goes on.

Every form, pattern, and motion in nature reveals that harmony is one of the basic laws of creation.

WILDERNESS SYMPHONY

WHO will write the symphony of the wilderness? What master with faultless ear will catch and pen that elusive melody to whose rhythm all nature moves? What soul so pure that it may rise to that realm "where the air is music" and gather into notes and measures the song of the forest—the song of the tides of verdure, the dance of hills and mountains, the metric march of seasons, the rhythm of erosion, the crescendo of the glacier, the cycle of bud and blade?

At times, when the heart is peaceful, faint strains of the sublime melody reach consciousness, though more felt than heard. One senses an understanding, an intimate knowledge of cause and purpose, which never can be explained. For the nonce he hears the universal harmony into which fits all nature, from tiny lichens to vast nebulae.

In moments rare and precious the writer has heard this song of songs and stood, perhaps as did the disciples at the Mount of Transfiguration, half-fearful at the perfection of the vision. Once he heard it on a remote hillcrest at sunset when brilliant pink streamers lined the western sky and the wild, sweet notes of a white-throated sparrow floated out from mysterious depths; once at night, in the Hemlock Colonnades on the Spring Lake Trail, when soft, silvered moonlight filtered through the delicate lacery overhead and speckled the forest floor with tangled shadows; once on a distant northern lake, beyond all man-made trails, when the Aurora danced in the blackened sky and sparkling Capella bathed in its ghostly waves; once by the white waters of the Ontonagon whose murmuring depths sang through the night like a celestial choir.

In these sacred environs he has heard the tom-tom of eternity, of which time is the audible beat. He has felt all nature—from the infinitesimal to the infinite—raising voice in one vast, glorious anthem.

The wilderness symphony opens with a prelude that is not a beginning and leads on through a finale that never ends. The song is from everlasting—only the auditor comes and goes. Dim in antiquity is faintly heard the divine theme of creation, first reaching the thoughts of man in whirling gases, molten rocks, seething vapors, and lifeless matter. But deep in this physical fortissimo are already heard the sweet promises of the life to come. (The first seas sang of the forests, of its peoples, and of man. All the vicissitudes of nature, all the illimitable unfoldment yet to come was foretold in this primitive

There is a source of wonderment
greater than stellar magnitudes,
the tricks of time,
or the miracle of growth.
It is that we are here
and have within us the ability
to know beauty, to be kind,
to experience patience, peace,
and deep piety.

theme whose origin is life's most beautiful mystery.) Elaborating, but never changing, the wilderness symphony expands, swells, and leads on through brilliant variations and exquisite climaxes. To the ancient roll of the sea are added the forest voices, the overtones of the winds, the voluminous hum of insects, the sound of hoof and wing, the hunting cry, the love call, the varying voice of man.

With equal beauty the eternal wilderness symphony softens to the dew shower or rises to the thrash of the tempest. "Life! Life! All is Life!" It sings of and through life's infinite forms. Its tender strains sound from under the blanket of snow, speaking as joyously of the falling seed as of the blooming flower, telling as much of life in the autumnal leaf shower as in the springtime bud. It sings with the same freshness of the arbutus this spring to bloom as of the ancient, ancient jungles, the rise and fall of continents, the creeping glaciers which came and went, leaving the lovely lakes as monuments and hoary shore-line forests to intrigue us with their rugged beauty.

What marvelous rhythm pervades this symphony. The lapping of the waves, the ebb and flow of tides, the cycles of sap, the phases of the moon, the tempo of day and year, the precession of the equinoxes—all move in perfect synchronism to the magic baton of the unseen Maestro.

The symphony sings with equal ease of dim past and distant future. It tells of the seed now planted which is predestined to grow into breath-taking beauty. It tells of forests that will wax and wane; flowers that will bloom and seed; fish, birds, and furred animals that will populate the waters and woods.

Changing but never ending; life rising out of life, ever evolving new beauty but never losing the old; singing eternally of the deep secret of existence, yet never divulging it; telling of the divine principle which animates all life from humble moss to towering sequoia, yet never explaining it—so the symphony of the wilderness plays on, unmindful of our attention, beautiful whether we open ear to it or not, perfect and purposeful despite our faulty understanding.

Cotton grass waves in the breeze, cotton clouds drift across the sky, a lovely languor rests on the landscape.

·§ SUMMER LAZINESS

SUMMERTIME wears laziness well. The mode just fits and goes perfectly with all the season's trimmings. Winter couldn't wear laziness—it would simply freeze to death if it did. And laziness wouldn't suit spring when there is so much to be done—all the snowdrifts to drain, planting to do, hoeing and plowing and raining and growing. But summer—why summer couldn't hurry if it wanted to, what with all the foliage, flowers, and fruitage it has to carry. And besides, it couldn't hear the birds if it went huffing, puffing about like autumn.

I have seen July go dawdling along, playing dreamily with its hot afternoons and warm romantic nights, as if it cared not a finger snap whether it got out of the way of the rest of the months or not. It seemed to spend all its time idly primping, combing out its green grasses, spreading out its leaves, tinting the flowers June had grown for it, and looking at its own image in lakes and festooned forest pools.

99

August has looked lazier still, brown with dried grass and gray with dust, but lacking sufficient ambition to take a shower bath. I have seen it let the flowers fade and its fields wither rather than rouse itself to sprinkle them. All it seemed to want was to sit still in the shade, too lazy to brush the flies off its forehead.

Summer is not only a season, it is a sensation. The world feels it in its very bones and sets to yawning and stretching. Summer is the fullest living with the least effort. It is the sea of mendicant leaves spread forth asking alms of the sun. It is the snooze on the north side of a haystack when heat is highest; the barefoot boy wishful thinking the time away beside a sluggish stream, his fishline tied to his toe. It is the deer lying on the shaded hillside, the homeless hobo clouds that drift in the sky, the breeze that wanders aimlessly north, south, east, or west—whichever direction is easiest.

Why, come to think of it, summer never bothers to come or go—it is just suddenly here, or gone. Spring comes. You can see its first approach in the awakening of bud and blade. Autumn comes, too, and works right hard at preparing for its colorful festival; and winter carries with it that ponderous carpet to spread over the earth. But with summer—well, one morning when spring has been around a while, you look out at a rising sun that is blazing hot, and there is summer, sitting all over everything. When it leaves, it is just as sudden. Perhaps it thumbs its way on the first cold wind, for there comes a morning when you look out and it is gone.

Imagination runs foot-loose in summertime, for it takes less effort to imagine than to know. Magic carpets were invented in this somnolent season. Then the forest is peopled with fairies, brownies, gnomes, and dwarfs that go sliding down moonbeams or ride astride a red-backed mouse. You can hear the tread of these little folk whenever a dewdrop falls on the forest floor. And yet no one has ever seen one of these tiny summer people because it is so much easier just to sit and dream about them.

There is a lesson to learn from the languor of summer. In the perfect play of creation there is a legitimate allowance for sabbaticals—for times when the highest virtue is just *being*. Human experience lists sad evidence that we mortals can *overdo* as well as *underdo* in this business of living. Often some of the doings of our fair fellows would have been better left undone. There is a reason for hammocks hung in the shade, for days spent in reading or in just thinking, for time allowed to slide by without being loaded with fantastic things fabricated of our fears and foolishness. Likely we need instill more summer spirit into our life design and learn the science of its lovely laziness.

He who would discover
the sacred secrets
of nature must be prepared
to trade ease and rest
for adventure. Ofttimes
the quiet hours of night,
so suited to sleep and dreams,
hold treasures of experience
that outvalue the luxury of repose.

A SLEEPLESS NIGHT

It was one of those humid nights when in the forest silence is added to silence, and all nature stands as if on the verge of some momentous event. August had come, and the frogs had ceased their wooing. The lakes were in bloom, fish languidly sought the deep holes, and the forests stood at the high tide of their summer glory.

Sleep is difficult on such a night; the potentialities are too great. And one must stay on guard, not against danger, but to capture adventure. There are experiences more restful than sleep anyway, and no reason why the healthy man should sacrifice many hours brimming with life to this overrated custom of repose.

I could not sleep on this August night. I found myself acutely sensitive to every forest sound, intently searching experience for their meanings, speculating as to what was happening then in some of my remote haunts. I felt that the wilderness was crawling with silent life. There did not seem to be enough sound to satisfy my hearing, and I strained through the silence to gather some distant voice that might have significance. For some hours I lay on my cot on the sleeping porch (misnamed that night), feeling that I was the auditor of a vast, unseen drama.

Some voices were familiar. Once I heard a loon, so far away his call was almost swallowed up by distance; a family of coyotes broke into one of their weird family quarrels, which lasted through an electrifying moment and then died away; again the cracking of twigs in the near woods brought pleasant but vain speculation. Everything was just outside the pale of my consciousness. I sensed this silent drama but could not grasp it.

My thoughts drifted idly from one subject to another: I reviewed the staggering measurement of Antares, glowing in the southern skies; I heard the fall of a pine cone and dwelt upon the long process which lay between its seed and the towering tree; I heard a mouse gnawing somewhere and prayed that he would go away before I had to trap him; I recalled a beautiful birch I had found once while wandering aimlessly in the unbroken forest back of us and promised I would search for it again; I thought of my friend who stood on the bow of a drifting boat and tried to jump to the dock, sending the boat back while he fell in the water, and I laughed aloud.

From deep in the woods now came a sound which commanded my attention. It was a cry I had never heard before—nor have I heard it since. In quality it

The owl has little time for sleep. His duty is to hunt and hoot—to be the nocturnal sentinel of the woodland.

was like the flat quack of a duck but had back of it the power of a larger creature. It was given at regular intervals, and obviously its author was coming closer, for it grew stronger. Others awakened in the cabin at the unusual sound, and questions were flashed back and forth, but none could identify the voice.

The cries were now coming from a point very near the lake, high in the treetops. I hurriedly dressed and found a flashlight. Next the call was directly overhead. The creature, which must be winged, was perching in our tall white spruce. I slipped out the door and made my way down the shadows, atremble with excitement—nature lore offers no greater thrill than the finding of a new creature. Soft but powerful wings whirred directly over me, and against the starlit sky I saw a bird of tremendous size. Uttering again its eerie cry, it alighted on our boathouse.

I worked my way toward it as slyly as possible and then suddenly caught it in the full ray of the flashlight. For only a moment I saw it—it took wing at once—but what a marvelous sight it was. A pure white bird, obviously of the owl family. I gasped in admiration as it spread its great wings and took to the air. Out into the night I traced its flight by the rhythmic harsh cry: for a moment it paused on the island, again at Brown Hill; I could hear it in the swamp beyond, and faintly on in the direction of Seven Mile Lake. I am not yet sure of its identity but believe it to have been the great arctic owl, which occasionally is seen this far south.

The great event had happened—that for which the forest was waiting had occurred. Sleep was now possible, though little of the night was left. The ghostly visitor had come and departed in mystery and darkness, keeping a secret tryst with nature and now returning to some exotic kingdom. The drama was at an end, the wilderness eased its tension, and wildlife resumed its habits. I heard the monotonous chirp of tree toads, here and there a cricket, and the first predawn call of the white-throat. I slept contentedly until the rays of the sun, already high, shone in my face, shaming my laziness.

In the midst of our praise
of unspoiled nature
let us remember the importance
of good companionship.
The joy of adventure
is doubled and redoubled
by the very presence
of one whose thoughts
are naturally akin to our own.

❧ MY PERFECT GUEST

My PERFECT guest came singing. I knew the moment he came rowing around the point of land which hides the Sanctuary from the passing world that I had invited the right man. His face was wreathed in smiles. He was truly happy to have come, and the fact that the boat which had been left for him at the road's end admitted large portions of the lake, wetting his feet and his baggage, failed to mar his good humor.

My perfect guest shook hands in a way that left no subtle doubt of his sincerity. He spoke of his joy in coming in a manner that was convincing and not gushing. He looked at our trees with a twinkle in his eye that showed me he could see beyond bark, leaves, and pulp into the soul of the tree itself.

It was a warm day, but my perfect guest uttered no complaint. He lifted some of his luggage without a grunt and permitted me to carry a bit of it without offending objections. He stopped for a moment to look down

Sunset Trail, saw in it that which I see—I know he
did, for he drew in a deep breath which savored of prayer
—and went into the cabin without comment. I was
grateful, my guest knew the *silent language*.

Mealtime came. I always sense some anxiety when
a new guest sits down to his first north-woods meal.
Urban variety is impossible in the woods unless one
makes this the object and forgets the forests. Would my
guest stand this test? Would he be a mass of grouchy
preferences? No, my perfect guest liked all things. He
liked them, not merely tolerated them; and while he
ate with an enthusiasm which was gratifying, his eyes
wandered adoringly over the distant shores of the lake.

My perfect guest bore no horror of mosquitoes,
though the trail swarmed with them. He did not tire
easily; but when he did tire, he plainly enjoyed it. He
entered each activity with obvious joy, rising to both
work and play with the same happy smile. If there was
wood to chop, dishes to wash, a meal to cook, he swung
into the task with a song on his lips. Never once did I
feel that he was making a sacrifice to aid with our routine. "There is no separation of tasks," said he. "Life
is all of a piece. That which we call work and that which
we call play are of one substance—I love it all."

I never needed to artificially inflate my guest's enthusiasm. I needed not to coat the dawn and sunset
with wordy praise. He knew the beauty that was there,
and I knew that he knew. I saw him caress the tiny
balsam and step aside to keep from injuring a violet. I

One need never be lonely
in the great outdoors.
There is satisfying companionship
to be found among forest folk
when we are worthy.
Even the common skunk,
when free of fear, becomes
the most agreeable creature,
despite his reputation.

heard him speak baby talk to our tame rabbits and chipmunks and saw him follow with intense enthusiasm
evidence of the beaver's intelligent activity.

Dusk came one evening in perfect calm. It was a
condition no canoe enthusiast could resist. I suggested
a canoe ride—and now my perfect guest finished his
conquest of my heart. "I had been hoping for this invitation," he said. "I want to cruise these shores with
you."

I knew from his first grip of the paddle that he
was not a stranger to the canoe. There is a great deal of
genuine affection shown when a canoe enthusiast takes
a paddle in his hand. He looks at it, turns it over, tries
its balance, and generally calls it a good paddle whether
it is or not—and means it. My perfect guest did just
this, and then set the paddle gently in the water, stroking with a skill which did not even tilt the canoe.

We paddled in perfect synchronism from the first,
and he hummed a few measures of a song, telling me
more plainly than words that he loved what we were
doing. A loon circled over the lake calling its praise of
the wilderness, and I watched my guest. Was he sensitive to these deeper charms? Did he understand the
native tongue of the forest? He ceased paddling, looked
overhead in the direction of the sound, and followed
the loon with his gaze until it had been swallowed up
in the distance. Then he began stroking again, showing
me by his silence that he really understood. A deer
started up from the shore, snorting back at us as he ran

through the woods, and I heard my guest chuckle softly. A whippoorwill sang incessantly from back in the forest, and a great bullfrog began his bass solo; an osprey, circling above, called constantly, and tree toads voiced their unending monotone. "It is all here," said my guest softly, "not one part is lacking."

There were broken motors, and my guest helped fix them; there were plans for pleasure which had to be abandoned; there was time consumed in obtaining supplies, and delays that ate up precious hours. But never did my guest complain or show impatience. He saw the humorous side in all things, rejoiced in difficulties, was ready of wit and sharp in repartee. He was intelligent but unsophisticated, took no pride in argument, yet ever sought true knowledge of the woods.

When the time came to go away, he met it manfully. He delayed his departure to the last possible hour, then left singing the same song he used on his arrival. I was sorry to see him go. The evening was heavy after that, and I went to bed early to hide from loneliness in sleep.

Clouds, strange ornaments of skies,
modeled of the mists,
what nature lover has not
flown aloft in fancy
to climb your cavernous sides
and to work with the winds
at molding your vaporous substance
into fading forms and figures!

~§ *CLOUDS*

WE HAVE been a bit unkind to clouds in our everyday metaphors. Just as we have used the dark loveliness of night to picture the gloom of our poorly directed thinking, so we have made these floating forms of vapor symbols of adversity. If the poet or philosopher speaks of a cloud drifting across the horizon of consciousness, we know from the habits of our speech that trouble is at hand. But we have no right to paint these heavenly wanderers with the pigment of our fears and despairs. The cloak of praise and beauty fits them better.

Perhaps some clouds are easier to love than others. Those which carry lightning on their brow, whose hair is ruffled with wind, and whose voices rumble ominously may challenge our fears. Others of milder character, which seem to exist only to add beauty to the sky, engage our thinking unaccompanied by imagined threat.

I am grateful that a wise mother, whose heart was so large she loved everything made by the Creator, taught me early to still my own fears and look more clearly upon omnipresent beauty. I remember now how, when I was quite a child, she would take me by the hand and lead me to a spot where we could see an approaching storm. Across the farm-strewn prairies of Illinois where we lived would drift shadows of those ponderous cumulo-nimbus clouds in whose caverns the lightning loves to play. "Thunderheads," we called them. I knew children who would hide themselves in fear when these heavenly monsters appeared, accompanied by the martial music of gigantic, hidden kettledrums. But my mother would permit me to form no such complex. She would point out the sheer beauty of the sprays of lightning, and she would find strength and grandeur in the rolling thunder that followed. She directed my attention to the misty streams of rain trailing through the distance, which probably would be upon us soon. She found never a threat in the storm, never anything to fear. Where the fluid fingers were touching, flowers would grow and the farmer's crops would prosper.

So, from the beginning of my education, I have learned to love clouds—all kinds of clouds. They were sort of playthings of mine. I couldn't touch them, of course, couldn't mold them or arrange them, but I could toy with them in my imagination. Hence, when I find them likened to troubles, I feel it somewhat a personal affront.

In the early days of summer when the cool and warm currents of air are vying for supremacy, the cumulus and strato-cumulus clouds are at their best. Great floating islands they are, their earthsides relatively smooth and of even altitude, while their boiling peaks stretch high into the heavens. Sometimes they look like huge buffaloes lazily grazing in the endless fields of blue heaven. They seem to typify the lazy dreaming invited by these first warm days. Like our thoughts on such a day, they go nowhere and yet neglect nothing by being as nondirectional as they are. They are the fitting mood of the moment: harmless idleness, visible spring fever, beautiful patience incarnate.

I have watched these clouds through the years. In barefoot days I have stubbed my toe on stones as I walked along looking up at them. From atop a haystack, from a drifting boat on a lazy Illinois river, from the bank of a winding clay-colored creek, through the leafy infinitude of graceful elms, I have seen and loved these ethereal "buffaloes." And today I look upon them with undiminishing adoration—and stub my toes as in days of yore. I like to search for faces in them as they forever try their skill at sculpturing. They have a preference for historical figures, and seldom a day passes that they do not model Washington, Lincoln, or Franklin.

There is a kind of cloud that looks like whiskers that have become separated from their parent chins. "Tufted cirrus," according to the international system of cloud classification; but they look like just plain white whiskers. They ride rather high, as clouds go, living at about fifteen thousand feet, and generally prefer to be the only clouds in the sky. There is quite a cluster at one end of this kind of cloud (where the whiskers once fastened to a vanished chin) and from this cluster stretch out dainty lines that become more and more tenuous until it is difficult to tell where the cloud leaves off and the sky begins. "Whisker-clouds" never hurry. They like to look leisurely about them as they go. Perhaps they understand how their presence makes the blue sky still more blue, and they strive to prolong the lovely effects.

Often following the "whisker-clouds," in time to make the sunset grand, comes the gossamer cirro-stratus, looking like frail spider webs drifting high in the heavens to catch the most delicate rays the sun has to give.

Another type of cloud formation seems to have been invented to complete the dramatic beauty of dawn. "Alto-cumulus," it is named, or more commonly "mackerel clouds." Perhaps some of the beauty is lost on those who dislike rain, for precipitation often follows these clouds. But they love to bathe in the rich red rays of the rising sun, rendering heaven and earth ineffably lovely in their glow. I have seen them spread the gold of dawn from horizon to horizon and hold it in ever growing brilliance until the sun itself climbed to the throne of day. Mackerel clouds are clumpy or mottled. Some poets have likened them to great flocks of sheep. They march steadily along, usually trailing a storm in their wake. They are always beautiful, but this charm reaches its zenith in the magic light of dawn.

The showy lady-slipper
is strictly a stylist.
Proud of her membership
in the aristocratic orchid family,
she comes brilliantly gowned.
The lowlands are her haunts,
her gaudy dress a startling contrast
to her somber surroundings.

There is another cloud effect so dramatic and so startlingly beautiful that it will cause most everyone to stop and look up in admiration. This is the cumulus roll, a ponderous, suddenly formed cloud which marks the heavenly meeting of a cool current of air and an existing warm area. It may portend a local thunderstorm, but not always. However, right where the cold and warmth meet will be formed this great, elongated roll, several miles in thickness and perhaps the width of a state. For sheer grandeur, for dramatic action, this cloud excels all others. Frequently the beauty is enhanced by its message, for it tells those who have had enough of heat that in all probability a cool change is at hand. Its volume is staggering to thought. It is not merely a mountain in the sky, it is a whole range of mountains!

Now what of the gray skies—the clouds that reach the limits of east, west, north, and south without a break through which the sun may shine or the blue sky be seen? Are they beautiful? Yes, they are beautiful, though perhaps their beauty is more difficult to define.

A gray sky rules at the hour this is being written and rain is falling. It is likely that this dullness of light and the rain will continue throughout the day. But the rain-beaded, dripping leaves of the birch trees outside my window have a new luster to them, a richer happier green. The ferns and tiny balsams on the ground, swaying as raindrops hit them, have a kind of beauty not before discerned. I hear the happy crackle of a gratefire, which would not be burning if the sun were shining.

Books and music, long neglected, will find joyful attention under the spell of this gray sky.

A gray sky beautiful? Yes, it is. I would not want it forever, but I need not fear, for nature loves variety and her mood will change. Right now it is good and timely to look up through dripping pine needles to a gray sky. There is a somber loveliness to it that makes it the grandest thing that could happen at the particular time in which it comes.

No, it is not meet that we should libel clouds by symbolizing in them our dark moods and miseries. For as they reflect the rosiest rays of the sun, so they should mirror back to us our happiest thoughts on their form and purpose.

It takes something of everything to make a day: a bit of beauty and joy, a portion of love, a seed of faith.

MORNING, NOON,
AND NIGHT

THE sun rose, it was morning.

But the sunrise alone did not make the morning. Every sound, shade, shadow, movement, and scent found in the vast agglomerate called nature was part and particle of the event. Bullfrogs were finishing in fading finale their nightlong symphony, and a hungry old pickerel fed savagely among them, sending whispering whirls of water through the lily pads. Cold gray clouds reached across the sky, ghostlike in the early dawn, then blushed with life as the newborn day approached. An old crow winged his way through the sky to unknown but definite destination, spacing his flight with an occasional "caw." A deer made his way rhythmically through the brush in perfect harmony with the surroundings, nipping a leaf here and there as he went. His dainty hoofs softly whispered as they autographed the sand at the water's edge; he paused to drink, looked solemnly out on the lake, then unhurriedly entered the forest again.

The bird chorus greeted dawn, the exquisite coloratura work of a linnet climaxing the prelude. A great blue heron flew up from his statuelike pose in the shallow waters, awkward until he got under way, yet graceful as any bird that flies once he had established the pattern. His harsh voice echoed on the shores and was answered by some invisible companion. A weasel wormed his way through the tangled mass of roots along the shore. A snake, little loved because little understood, glided through the grass. Aspen leaves danced in a light morning breeze, hilltops sang in the sunshine, pine trees bowed a stately greeting as the winds gained strength, wavelets raced across the lake, shadows scurried from the forest.

All these things, and a million more, make the morning. Yet it would not be complete were there no human heart to respond in love, no human heart to say, "What infinite glory, this! What indisputable evidence of the goodness of creation that I, who am conscious of all this, am an indispensable part!"

The sun was at the zenith, it was noon.

But the position of the sun alone did not make the noon. The world shimmered in lively light. Trees spread their leaves widely to catch the heavenly manna which descended upon them. Birds somewhat silenced their songs, but the very air glowed with the beauty of their presence as they flew, hopped, and climbed about in their feeding. Hawks toyed with the air currents, riding them in effortless flight, while the small creatures of the forest sought safety in brush and burrow. Chipmunks darted from cover to cover, busily stuffing their cheeks with seeds. Red squirrels raced miraculously from tree to tree, pausing now and then to chatter a challenge to any and all who would dare enter their woodland realms.

Deer searched out a secret retreat along the edge of a swamp and here rested, waiting for the comparative safety of dusk and darkness. A graceful osprey flew low over the lake, then suddenly dived into the water, appearing an instant later with a moderate-sized fish in his talons. From high overhead an eagle dropped down, loudly challenging the right of the osprey to his catch, and, the argument still unsettled, the two birds disappeared beyond the horizon.

A bear and an old porcupine met, and while the bear wisely kept his distance, the porky climbed a maple tree and made himself comfortable in a high crotch. Waves roughly played with the shores, flowers reflected their gratitude to smiling skies, lazy white clouds drifted across the blue, pines murmured in increasing winds, while oaks, maples, birches, and aspens danced spiritedly.

Of such things is made the noon. And to the listening ear nature says, "Life and its expression—living things—forever have strength equal to any occasion. Morning promises noon—noon with its opportunity, its tasks, its demands. Stand up bravely, happily, to the world before you. That which seems to challenge is but the shadow of your own ability and strength, offering a field for expression. You love the morning, love also the noon."

The sun had set, it was night.

But the disappearance of the sun did not make the night. The western sky had been a blaze of colorful glory, and the light of day had held long in the north-western sky as though reluctant to leave. The wind of noon came to rest as shadows gripped the forest, and all nature knelt in that sacred hour of prayer which intervenes between daylight and dark.

Wavelets ceased their boisterous play and lost their identity in the mysterious calm of the lake. The great blue heron had returned to his feeding ground and now stalked along gracefully as he made his evening meal of crab, fish, frogs, and minnows. A hermit thrush re-estab-lished his reputation as the forest's greatest musician by sending his unmatched song into the still air.

Far back in the forest the voices of several coyotes broke forth. Frogs again launched their lay, fish leaped into the air, a hoot owl called, robins murmured their sleepy song, and two loons played insanely along the surface of the water. The deer were again afoot. Meteors streaked the heavens, a moon arose to dim the stars, northern lights reached filmy fingers aloft, trees became silent shadows. A wildcat slipped cautiously to the still waters for a cooling drink and was promptly made un-welcome by the splashing of a beaver.

These are the ingredients of night, together with un-numbered more. And out of this medley the receptive heart hears this message: "Love this season of repose. Think not that peace and rest are idleness. It is in this tranquillity, this silence and solitude that you know best what you are. When you better understand your being, you better direct your doing. Here learn the permanence of creation, cast aside your futile, vain ambition, cease your aimless striving. Learn the pace of the universe which is ever constant, and seek not to race ahead or yet to drag behind. A new day has been added to your experience. It is not past or is it lost, but is now yours forever. Beyond this lovely night comes another morning, another noon, and yet another night. It will always be so. Therefore, set your stride for eternity; abandon your will in favor of the universal order of things; and know only one duty: to look in wonderment at the endless unfoldment of infinite creation."

Fear is the screen
that hides from our view
the friendship native
to the wild heart.
Wildness is only a form of fear,
for when kindness and patience
have penetrated the veil,
we see unmistakable evidence
of the love in all forms of life.

FRIENDSHIP

FRIENDSHIP is a deep subject, perhaps the most influential in the lexicon of mankind. It is deserving of frequent, serious, and unemotional consideration, for there is not a person, a community, or a nation that does not have life influenced by friendship. Perhaps my thoughts on it are a bit unorthodox. I hope they are not offensive to the high idealism held by many, for certainly they come from years of careful thought.

I cannot conceive friendship as being merely the personal relationship of one human being to another. It is vastly greater than that. Friendship, when purified of selfishness, is the highest form of love we see in this world. Even the home is more dependent upon a spirit of friendship between homemakers than upon flaring, emotional love. It is friendship that lifts the barriers between parents and their children and curtails the restraining, consuming affection often mistaken for love, but which is merely subtle selfishness.

Friendship dulls the edge of sharp competition in business and leads to an attitude which would provide room for all. Friendship would lead capital to understand labor, labor to understand capital, nation to understand nation, and all to see that we only gain liberty as we give it and only have love as we live it.

Friendship is not in the friend—it is too glorious for that. It is the atmosphere of heaven enveloping earth. As the sunlight it shines upon us, and we are glorified in its radiance. But it does not arise from us, nor does it die within us. It is a divine quality, for its beauty is ever a sharp reprimand to worldliness and commonplace thinking; it is a quality of immortality, for though the friend may depart, friendship remains forever, finding expression and giving solace.

I have felt friendship so many places and under so many circumstances in this world that I look upon it as a spiritual quality pervading all life. I have looked upon friendly skies in the north, and when lost, followed the pointing fingers of friendly stars to safety. To understand them was to find their friendliness. I have found the woodland's friendly protection from the elements and crouched in the shelter of its trees to escape heat, rain, and cold; to understand the forest was to find its friendliness. I have found the creatures of the woods most anxious to demonstrate friendship and most happy to find it reflected in me. Understanding alone discovered this in them. Always, as my understanding increases, I see more of real friendship revealed in the world about me, in the people, creatures, and things that combine to populate this good old universe.

As to human friends—and oh, I thank God for them —I am sure we do both friend and friendship an injustice when we clutch at them and make our love consuming, restraining, and limiting, rather than a liberation of affections. Wise Emerson warns that if we would have friends, we must be able to do without them. Yet our unwise sentiments will often cry to the friend, "If I could not have you, I would die."

Anything which leans upon another is a burden, and the friend who leans upon a friend is no exception. I shudder to think of the weight I cast upon friends before I learned that. And I shall never forget the glorious release it was to me, and to them, when out of solitude came the lesson to me that I must be complete within myself or be accounted unworthy of friendship.

Another injustice committed in the name of friendship is that of setting standards for those we name friends. Too often we deny them the opportunity of actual self-improvement—that growth that comes of solving individual problems—by believing them more advanced in their evolution than they really are. Just because I love my friend is no reason that I should think him a superior being, especially when to do so makes him unnatural in my presence and suspends him at an altitude from which he must one day descend.

I shall never forget the shock that was mine when a grand old friend said to me, "My boy, you think too highly of me, and I want you to stop it. It is too great a handicap and makes me really want to escape from you." The sublime honesty of that! We have been better friends ever since, and we enjoy greater liberty.

It is true that we are prone to judge others by what they do, ourselves by our intentions. Particularly do we do this with our friends. We say, when the moment of trial comes, "Well, I did not think you would ever do *that*," or "You have disappointed me." But what right do we have to set laws for their behavior or so to design their lives that we are subject to disappointment? No, if we want to realize something of the true glory of friendship, we must strip the smallness from it. I was adrift alone in a canoe at the Sanctuary one wonderful evening when this realization came to me anew, and with it came an overwhelming sense of gratitude for friendship wherever I find it.

Always understanding is associated with its revelation. I have seen it in the stray dog when I offered him a bite to eat, a few words of kindness, and a pat on the head. I have seen it in the creatures at the Sanctuary as they realize that they are understood—and loved. I have seen it in fellow men, singly and in multitudes, and I see it more and more as I learn to understand all better. I have found that the more I use of friendship the more I have of it; that I can love all mankind without lessening the love I have for those most intimate with me; and that I can permit friends the liberty to love all without losing any of that which I call mine.

Friendship is like the atmosphere. It is something in which we "live and move and have our being," and it will outlive all our petty, small, and selfish notions about it. It is God's most precious gift to the world—and sometimes it is whispered within me that it is even God Himself revealed!

Every nature lover knows the true treasure of the wildwood is that which the heart seeks and finds.

⊷ HIGHER FINANCE

THE capriciousness of investment convulses the world. Commercial paper and properties with fixed or constantly advancing values appear as an illusion comparable to Ponce de León's Fountain of Youth. A mere whim of chance and the highest securities diminish in worth, making all material fortunes seem purely hypothetical.

The fundamental basis on which the worth of an investment must be judged is the net return to the investor. It is not enough to judge it merely by the interest rate. Though it might ultimately pay out a substantial dividend, if its incidental fluctuations have been the instigator of uncertainty and worry, the net result to the investor is a loss. The final worth of any investment is relative to its effect on peace of mind.

Some years ago the writer took the last cent he possessed and made a trip into the north country. In later years he experienced varying fortunes and prosperity.

Investments were made in diverse stocks and various enterprises, all of which, in the honest analysis, were a loss. Yet the investment in the northern trip has never missed a dividend! Every delightful hour spent in the great woods is still a fresh memory, brightening conversations, inspiring plans, and ever furnishing a potential escape from an imposing world. Spirit, mind, and body still feast on the benefits of this and other journeys into the land of lakes, woods, and peace.

True, this reasoning would have no collateral value with a banker. That is because it is nonnegotiable—it is of such personal and permanent nature that it cannot be transferred or lost. It has a higher value than is recognized by the banker or, perhaps more properly, by banking. A bank credit might temporarily lift financial pressure, defer it until a later date, but the investment in nature happiness will reveal the only avenue of escape from the whole category of commercialism.

One troubled year a guest came to the Sanctuary of Wegimind. He was laboring under the general conditions of financial depression and had left behind him a sweltering, seething, competitive city. For a few days he wandered the forest trails and drank in the cool peace of northern evenings. "One thing I have learned," he said later, "is that there is no depression in nature—trees are just as beautiful, bird songs just as sweet, fishing just as enticing, dawns and sunsets just as brilliant, and the cool, bracing air of the northern forests is just as salubrious as ever!"

The fascinating old black bear is a very sensible fellow.
When winter comes, he takes a nap until it all blows over.

Spiritual prosperity knows no business cycles or periodic waverings. Investments made to this end are of a security which cannot depreciate. The money placed in a summer home, in boats, tents, or cameras and the time spent outdoors, all pay the investor a dividend which cannot be omitted or deferred.

The larger lesson of a world depression is that we should make a distinction between financial values and real values. When riding on the high waves of postwar prosperity, man lost his sense of values. Consideration of fellow men, appreciation of home ties, love of the ethical and beautiful ran at low tide. While stock profits were built high, progress in character was negligible. Man became intoxicated with the spirit of accumulation. In a twinkling this false condition was swept from him, and he saw that his storehouses were packed with shadows. At the highest moment of his material prosperity he was spiritually impoverished. Spiritual values are the real values, and life conducted on any other basis is as a "house built upon the sands." The presence of fabulous wealth has never given happiness where it has been gained at the sacrifice of character. Ultimately investment will be judged from only one standpoint: its contribution to mental progress and peace of mind.

High finance may twist the fortunes of communities and nations, and a distrustful race result; but higher finance will take into the accounting man's spiritual welfare and lead to happiness. One may well do without expensive motorcars, elaborate mansions, costly raiment and jewels; he may do without high office and financial dominion over men; but he cannot do without thoughts of beauty, peace, kindness, reverence, and love. He may do without social pomp and display, but he cannot do without the heart-satisfying sincerity found in the gatherings of honest, good-humored folk about a flickering campfire. He may do without costly travel to distant places, amid castles and famed resorts, but he cannot do without the simple, quiet walks through avenues of celestial trees. He may do without his highly opinionated self which struts before men, but he cannot do without the humble, adoring self he is when he walks with nature and with God!

Among the woodland creatures
there are many who see well
in the rays of darkness
and have learned to love
night better than day.
The canny old raccoon is one
who has chosen to dwell
in ebony mansions, and he is
master of his environment.

EBONY MANSIONS

THERE are those who, through traditional fear of darkness, miss the silent glories of the night. Perhaps it was well for our race in primitive days to seek refuge at the first suggestion of dusk; but those were days of mental darkness. The torch of intelligence has revealed to us many new, lovely mansions of nature, not the least of which is her spacious palace of ebony.

Night magnifies our vision, rather than limits it. Whereas in daylight we see but one star—the sun—whose light reaches us in some eight minutes of impetuous travel, in darkness we see thousands of stars, or suns, from which light must journey many years to reach us. We are confined to our solar orbit by daylight; our realm is infinite by night!

All nature is decorously quieted by the cloak of darkness. Voices are involuntarily softened, moves are gentle and slow, and thoughts are rendered tranquil. Looking into the immensities of interstellar space, man is reminded how insignificant he is in physical comparison, yet how great in his spiritual and intellectual endowments which enable him to comprehend something of this grandeur.

The little creatures of the forest love night. No sound in all the vast repertory of nature is more inspiring than the flutelike tones of the hermit thrush when it has retired to its secret chamber and casts back its beautiful farewell to the day. And who has not thrilled at the happy call of the whippoorwill as he skims the treetops? Or the wild, sweet notes of the esoteric, white-throated sparrow breathed into the nocturnal extravaganza? Had one no eyes to see the charms of the wilderness, he could know it all from the song of the whitethroat. If the hermit thrush is the soul of the woods, the whitethroat is its spirit!

Highly treasured in our hearts is the memory of one heavenly night when inspiration led us to ground our canoe at the Spring Lake Trail. Big Fork Lake seemed a clear window to infinity that night, for below us in the mirrorlike waters the heavens were reflected as.massive and perfect in form as above. A dainty sliver of a new moon hung low over the far shore, and close by hovered Venus, of unprecedented brilliance—as if trying to outshine her ancient rival. Again the inverted scene in the waters was equal in perfection to the original, until distorted by the wake of the canoe. (Is not this philosophically true: that the beauty of perfection is always present and apparent though our vision may be deformed by undulations of our own creation?)

A deer contested our right on the trail through the Hemlock Colonnades that night. We caught his glowing eyes in the far-reaching rays of the flashlight. He pawed the ground in his disapproval, turned his lovely head from side to side trying to understand the light, and occasionally snorted to rid his sensitive nostrils of the dread odor of man. He tolerated our presence for a few minutes, then to show his nonchalance, nipped a tender leaflet from a nearby birch and moved off into less public chambers of his sylvan palace. He was not frightened—rather offended—and we could trace his slow movements by their sound, far into the dark woods.

Infinite is the forest at night. Our presence made but a tiny bubble of light in this sphere of darkness. We moved up the trail and over the ridge of young birch. The birch is the lady of the forests, the poet says—and milady wore sparkling jewels in her hair that night.

We sat for a time on a large log which bars the trail and drank of the deep stillness. Not far away some little animal hustled about in the dry leaves. How sounds are magnified in this setting! At a distance there was a heavy crash as some sorely tried limb finally gave way and fell to the ground. Such an innovation in solitude is startling, and it is well to be a little apprehensive if you would gain the greatest joy of night in the woods. One knows that it is no threatening beast or goblin, but it is well to leave open the possibility.

The silence is deepened after a loud noise, perhaps because one tries harder to hear the something he knows is not there. We sat intently listening for some time, until our efforts were rewarded. We heard voices, many of them, far ahead in the darkness. They were human voices in merry mood—shouting, laughing, calling names and messages which we could not quite catch. But by the tones we knew them to be friendly souls indulging in the most joyous repartee. The voices were mixed: some high pitched as of women and some the baritones of men. One moment they seemed to be approaching, the next farther away. Several times we thought our names were called, but we were not sure.

We were not long mystified. I knew those friendly voices, knew them and loved them ever since those boyhood days when I first heard them on the elm- and willow-lined rivers of Illinois. They were the voices of the woods, which the Indians call the *voyageurs*.

Do not analyze the voices of the woods too acutely, or they disintegrate. Let them have their mystery. They are more charming in the occult than in the familiar. Let them be eerie babblings of forest spirits, and we the unsuccessful eavesdroppers. Whatever their meeting, it is festive; whatever their message, it is good; whatever their realm, it is behind the impenetrable wall of nature, and we must look in adoration on this side, while they gaze joyously on the other. We shall never look upon them or catch a single word they say, though in each silent moment it seems we are at the point of doing so.

We moved on down the trail, in the direction of the voices, but they promptly retreated. We came to the perfect oval which is Spring Lake and looked in renewed awe at the reflected heavens. Night birds called through the darkness. From far beyond, where Capella toyed with the silhouetted treetops, came the sporadic outburst of a family of coyotes. A gentle breeze rustled the sensitive aspens; a swell of unknown origin broke in tiny wavelets on the shore; an owl asked "who-o-o" we were; and meteors made fading marks in the sky.

It seems regrettable that one cannot forever stay at this point of extreme sensitiveness and high appreciation. The beauty of the Infinite lifts us spiritually aloft; our weighty thinking pulls us down. One must come away from scenes which charm and must rest from the mood which enchants. But these foretastes of heaven are waymarkers, leading to patience with the world and faith in the ultimate.

Night has been much defamed. It has been used to symbolize adversity and despair. But night shines with a glory all its own, and in its silent hours has come to man the greatest inspiration. "By night, an atheist half believes a God," says Young. No one can remain insensible to the vastness of creation as he looks into space by the light of darkness. There is a rich reward awaiting the receptive soul who breaks the traditional tethers of the fireside and steps forth to view nature with his eyes freed of blinding light.

145

Trees are skilled ministers, for they preach not but point thought to messages of truth already in the heart.

·⋖§ *TREES*

The groves were God's first temples . . . . Ah, why
Should we, in the world's riper years, neglect
God's ancient sanctuaries, and adore
Only among the crowd, and under roofs
That our frail hands have raised?

THUS wrote the poet Bryant of that supreme, inexplicable miracle we call the forest. "God's ancient sanctuaries," indeed! And today if they are held at lower
level in our esteem, the error lies in concept and not
in any possible depreciation.

In the halls of these verdant temples the soul of the
thinking man is filled with wonderment. He is over-
awed with evidence of the magnitude and unfathomable
depths of creation. He is inundated with miracles. Life
itself is a miracle, as deep and mystifying in the shy
violet as in the hoary white pine; as startling in the
instincts of the tiny ant as in the forest wisdom of the

ponderous moose. For from microscopic organisms to orbits of galaxies, all life moves to laws not of its invention, which attest to the infinite power and intelligence of the Creator of all.

What more fitting place of worship than the forest where there is such multiform evidence of Him whose name is Love! What greater heresy than to violate these sanctuaries which the hands of man cannot again fashion.

Trees have been a haven for man throughout his history. In his humble, earthly beginning he fled to them for protection from enemies mightier in body than he. He sought food from their branches, he lay in their shadows out of the blazing sun, he crept into their hollows for shelter. As intelligence grew, he shaped their branches into weapons, hollowed their trunks into canoes, and found solace, warmth, and protection in fires kindled of their fiber. He built dwellings of them far superior to his gloomy caves, fashioned vehicles to lighten his burdens, made paper on which to record his thoughts, and found food and medicine in the very lifeblood of his arboreal guardians.

Then he found buried treasure deep in the earth that trees of other ages had left for him. He came to learn that the roots of the forests hold the very earth in shape; that they foster nourishing rains, yet prevent floods and soil erosion.

And now as man stands abashed at the vacuum of materiality, these tireless mentors furnish him with spiritual guidance. Their beautiful fingers point his thoughts aloft, away from earthly concepts. Where man once saw in them but objects of utility, he now finds beauty and inspiration. Surely, surely this feathery green covering which spreads over the world and its life is the protecting wing of the Almighty! A tree is, indeed, a faint slit in the veil, through which shine some of the glories of heaven.

The very law, order, beauty, and harmony of the universe is the visible evidence of an Invisible Governor.

๛ GOVERNMENT

TRUE government is not fully represented in a tangled morass of human laws, competitive legislative groups, or the clash of selfish interests. Look into the star-filled heavens some clear night. *There* is a better, truer symbol of government.

See the immeasurable skies dotted with stars that circle in orbits they have not designed, stars propelled by power they did not originate, obeying laws they did not invent. And note that the result is one of beauty and peace. Look into the dark mass of trees which hover about the cabin as a warming, protecting blanket; out of the primitive seed they came, growing upward by an impulse they cannot speed or retard, revealing a glory they dare not call their own. And see that through their very naturalness, their unresisting obedience to invisible government, the result is tranquillity.

Look to the planet we live upon: mountains rising with unmatched ease, rivers carving valleys with unequaled patience, winds tirelessly spreading moisture about the earth, continents rising and falling with less effort than man exerts to lift a feather. And always that which we see is governed by something unseen.

True government rises from regions into which we see not, and the laws of these regions offer the only road to peace and plenty. For as these laws achieve tranquillity in the universe, so can they work in the realm of mankind. But we differ from the things about us in that we are conscious beings. It is within our capacities to become conscious of this Divine Government and to gain happiness through understanding it.

From time to time throughout history there have been those so free of the mists of selfishness that they perceived and revealed something of the unseen government and the laws which direct us to progress. "Do unto others as you would have them do unto you," is one revelation of divine decree; another of like nature is "Love thy neighbor as thyself;" and others include, "Thou shalt not kill," "Thou shalt not steal," "Thou shalt not bear false witness," "Thou shalt not covet."

Who with any claim to wisdom can say that such government of human affairs would not lead to that state of freedom and happiness we seek, and who can say with any truth that there is any other way to attain it? Human systems of government are commendable and successful in the degree that they reflect this Divine Government—they are failures, no matter what their name and nature, where they deviate from it.

The woodchuck, homely but appealing,
obeys in his own original way
the laws which govern creation.
He is alert, courageous, industrious
and builds his remarkable underground home
with provision for security,
comfort, and sanitation.

In a beaver colony we find no bosses, no ruler, no dictator. Each animal works diligently, anxiously, willing to fight, not to get out of work but to do it. He refuses to be deprived of his share of service to the colony. He needs no urging, no threat of penalties, no promise of personal reward. And the result is that a beaver colony in undisturbed wilderness exists with a minimum of misery and difficulty. It is closer in some ways to the unseen government than we are.

There is no short cut to the utopia we picture, nor is our vision an impossible dream. The yearning for perfection is but the call of perfection. Yet that grand unfoldment comes only through living in accordance with the laws of God so clearly revealed in Christianity. Who can point out one error in government which could not be corrected by applying the sterling principles, or one fond ambition of the human heart which could not be quickly realized by the same simple process?

True government begins with the individual and spreads to nations; it does not originate with national systems and reach down to the individual. We yearn for peace and prosperity and look to national and international legislation to give these to us. We have looked in this direction throughout our history, yet today have less of that which we seek than when we started. We have looked everywhere for right government—except within our own hearts! But until we do turn our thoughts inward and purify individual consciousness, our highest sounding theories, noblest motives, and complicated ruling systems are but mockeries.

Would war be possible if we loved our neighbors as ourselves? No—and a spirit of neighborly understanding would reap rich dividends. Could governments wallow in the filth of spoliation were the commandment "Thou shalt not steal" recognized? No—and only as this commandment is practiced is there any true profit. Would there be market crashes if we did unto others as we would have them do unto us? No—and the resulting prosperity would be enduring.

True government is forever coming to us out of that realm from which all things arise—and only as we recognize it will we find our haven. It is in solitude, in quiet communion with nature, that we reach most deeply into truth. Here we learn more of reality than all the high-charged words and fanatic gesticulations of political oratory can teach. We see that the first and last step of right government is in governing within ourselves· those mental evils which are the seed of life's difficulties. No national system is safe until this is done!

Nature is always just herself,
and the crowning feature
of her lovely landscapes
is pristine simplicity.
Hence, peaceful rest comes
when we dwell in her temples,
when we are led to cease
our tiresome pretending
and just be ourselves.

NATURALNESS

THE noble honesty of the wildwood is its fundamental charm. It permits no assumptions, offers no shams. A tree is just a tree, a flower just a flower—all content with their God-given beauty and worth, taking their rugged environment for granted, meeting it with all their endowed courage and power.

Among men one seldom meets with this ingenuousness—and this accounts in a manner for misanthropic leanings and preference for nature. But how appealing is naturalness when found in man. What greater joy does social life offer than meeting the man who speaks and acts freely from an unpretentious heart? The biographer, sorting out the episodes which will endear his subject to the public, wisely dwells more on his purely human traits—his affections, his loyalty, his humanity—than on his great public deeds. And most prized is the frank, honest smile and the freedom of speech and action which spring from a straightforward manner.

If you would know your friend, take him to the woods. In the city he may secrete his true self from you for years, but within the confines of a cabin or camp he has no place to hide. Trees will conceal a body, but they reveal character. Among the classes and types of the city, man may justify his pretenses by pointing to numerous models, but nature offers him no prototype. Nature is a kind of X ray, which looks one through and through, revealing true substance. A friend who proves companionable in the outdoors is a friend for life!

No fraternal order in the world is more closely knit than the brotherhood of the outdoors; no lodge is better supplied with shibboleths to identify its members. Meet a stranger, and with what suddenness the reserve melts at mention of the magic words—fishing, the cabin, the woods. Eyes light with a mystic twinkle, peculiar to the kind; chairs are drawn closer; and within a moment there is a competitive swapping of observations and experiences. And, as is always the case with one's own, you can't help but respect more deeply a man who loves the woods. There seems in it some guarantee of his honesty. A fisherman exhausts his misrepresentations in measuring the size of his catch—he is dependable in all other matters. Jesus of Nazareth chose his disciples from among fishermen.

Man stands judgment before nature. Among the pines he must stand as straight as they or be conspicuous in his hypocrisy. He seems, as it were, confronted with the spiritual truth of life, which he must either humbly

The simple yellow daisy,
or black-eyed Susan,
hides its bright beauty
by its very abundance.
Numerous along roadsides
and in meadows, it acts
as the eye of earth,
commissioned to watch
summer's changing skies.

accept or reject and flee back to his artificial playhouses where he is a fancied king in an imagined realm.

What sweet confidences flow over the campfire. Many a man has dug deeply into his heart and unloaded to a friendly and trustworthy listener a burden which became lighter in the telling. Entangled plans have been sped to clarity and dwarfed ambitions assuaged in the freedom of a campfire powwow. What grand release to talk without fear of being misunderstood or put at disadvantage. Sometimes it seems that we have lost heavily in the bargain when we exchanged our primitive sincerity for education, sophistication, and industrial mastery.

The Kingdom of Heaven will indeed be uncovered in the affairs of men when man stands and acts with the naturalness of trees, when he gives forth the fruit natural to his kind—good will, honesty, charity, kindness, and courage. Now we flee to the wildwood for our peace, where there are few men and many trees. But were man stripped of his falseness, were he the grand, lovable creature God created, finding him in great numbers would but multiply our joy. In truth, we are seeking in fellow man the accurate reflection of perfection we know underlies all appearances.

Instinctively we all know that the truly natural is the truly good. Our habits of speech testify to this. Our highest compliment to one we really admire is that he is perfectly natural. Such a tribute belongs only to the friend who is thoroughly dependable, whose word is his bond, who is without guile and deceit. This friend is free of strutting and pretense, his love and friendship unfeigned. He says what he means and means what he says, but his judgments are mellowed by compassion. His attitude and acts savor of kindliness, for he knows men are all of one blood and assumes no personal superiority. He wears old clothes without apology and new clothes without comment—and permits us to do the same. We feel no strain in his presence and no fear of gossip when he is gone.

Such a man is not a singularly gifted individual. He has only those spiritual qualities common to us all. But he *lives* his innate virtues, whereas others screen theirs and abide in invented substitutes. So we welcome his firm handclasp, his warm smile, the friendliness in his eyes, the medicine of his companionship; and as he walks away, we gaze after him and draw from our hearts our highest tribute, "Blessed fellow! He is perfectly natural."

Naturalness in its deepest sense is the criterion of worth in this world.

Nature ever amazes us,
doing the same old things
in new ways. How often
we have laughed at
the awkward pranks
of the black-bear cub,
yet the next one we see
will amuse us just as much
with his age-old routine.

EXHAUSTING THE NORTH

It is often difficult for a thoroughly urbanized person to understand how a nature lover can return to the same lakes and woods year after year without being surfeited or bored. The quest for variety has become a mania for those living in environs where the only interest is artificial stimulus created by restlessness. That the same trees, the same waters, the same moon should continually stir new ecstasy is inconceivable to such. Yet those who have turned to the sanctuary of nature for decades find that with each visit every element of the woods has been enhanced in beauty and importance.

If it is variety that the human mind craves, nature is in this a specialist. So precious is newness and individuality in the scheme of creation that not an object or a moment is ever duplicated. In all the flakes of snow, no two are found alike; there are no duplicates among the leaves of trees or the blades of grass. An exact reproduction of any unit is unknown to nature.

As with things, so with time. No moment is ever repeated. The earth never twice occupies the same point in infinite space, stars do not stand for even a fraction of a second in the same relationship to each other. All objects in the universe alter with each instant, never to return to any one station of their unending evolution. There is no stagnation in nature!

Yet the prophet could find "nothing new under the sun," nor can we! The unending appeal of the wildwood springs from its interesting development and man's ever broadening view.

Though the song of the wood thrush has rung forth clear as a bell countless times, it comes again with renewed sweetness, reaching thought with deeper meaning than ever before. The moon, parading through its phases during eons of time, has but gathered glory in the march and looks on each night with fresh-born beauty. Far-flung forests, majestic mountains, rolling hills, singing streams, and all the creatures that inhabit them are adorned by the touch of time—ever the same yet ever different.

Nature enters our experience differently with the passing years. On each upward step of progress we find waiting for us an entirely new side of the forests. To the impressionable boyish mind, which seeks outlets for its energies and objects for its fancies, the woods come decked in mystery. They flaunt a tantalizing challenge to dawning virility and instinct, calling from the budding man the latent powers which stimulate his growth. When this mind has matured and there are flickerings of wisdom where there were only enthusiasms before, the trees keep pace with development. The spreading oak which served boyish fancy as a playground answers adult thought when it begins to question more deeply. The forests become testimonials of the omni-presence of life and the symbol of freedom. The lakes are mirrors of heavenly beauty, and the world is wrapped in a garment heretofore unobserved—spirit. The vast north reveals infinite resourcefulness, staying ever abreast of man.

This will be the experience of the north-woods lover always, though he continues his visits without end. Not until he tires of the life-giving sunshine, will he tire of the north. Not until his soul wearies of beauty, his heart rejects love, and his mind rebels at peace, will the charm of the forest seem at an end. Time only waters its enchantment, constant return but multiplies its appeal.

Ofttimes imagination will unlock nature's doors, admitting us to realms unknown to reason and cold observation.

FROM AN OLD DIARY

I AM glad that I am not afraid to dream. I am glad that I see in every living, moving thing an expression of intelligence to be understood; recognize every nook and corner of the world as fertile fields for romance; and perceive in every manifestation of life, even my own thoughts and actions, the testimony of one all-pervading Mind expressing itself through infinite channels.

Trees are living, intelligent beings to me—and I am glad. I see them thoughtfully working out their problem, which is identical with my own—seeking light. They express in unmistakable language the qualities we most desire in man: courage, joy, virility, reverence, industry, and accomplishment. I hear their gentle murmurs as soft, whispered conversations, and at times I seem to understand what they are saying.

The forest aisles are strewn with romance for me. A hemlock grove is a series of beautiful colonnades in a boundless temple; the verdant halls of the forest are peopled with gnomes and veiled in delightful mystery; a hill or mountain is a gorgeous holy cathedral, its crowning rocks and trees inspired ecclesiastics. The club moss is the couch of gnomes, the ferns are the playgrounds of fairies. The flowers are the joyous song of Mother Earth, the humble weed a part of the refrain.

The stars are alive, close, friendly—and I am glad. They talk, sing, have purpose and human propensities. The sky is a vast dome roofing the universe; every point in it is approachable, reachable, understandable. The filmy gossamer of the Aurora is not an unexplained phenomenon to me but the signaling of spiritual beings.

Animals are individuals to me—and I am glad. I think of them not as slaves, serving man only with flesh and hide, but as copartners in the glorious revelation of the infinitude of life. I recognize their fears and loves akin to our own. I see them loving the right, yet restrained by fear even as man, and I perceive in their occasional ferocity the desperation of a mind that cannot fully understand, and is not wholly understood. An animal is important to me. I feel urged to help it with its problems and to bridge the gap between our worlds with kindness and sympathy.

I can see God reflected in man—and I am glad. I see evidence of the Almighty's hand in man's eternal tendency to rise higher and higher in the spiritual scale. This I see in that man should even want to love, to sacrifice for general good, to be honest, to be reverent, to grow in grace. I see in the lowest of men the same degree of divinity as in the highest, only buried more deeply in an error not his own. In all, great and small, praise God, I see a potential fountain of infinite worth and beauty which must some day free itself of old impediments and flow with unmeasured goodness.

Oh, I am glad I am not captured and enslaved by what some would call stern reality, into which are gathered only the sordid, tragic, and evil. I am glad I am not harnessed to the ground, fearful to look upon anything not of atomic structure. I am glad that my thoughts can rise above the clouds, look upon truths more solid than matter, sense the cause back of all effects and the joy in eternal sunshine, though my feet still rest in shadows. I am glad I am not afraid to dream!

Dusk is the interval
between the close of day
and the beginning of night,
into which nature gathers
her most subtle, precious charms.
Sweet silence creeps
over the forest world,
which stands with head
bowed in prayer.

❧ DUSK

Down through the starry intervals,
  Upon this weary-laden world,
How soft the soul of Silence falls!
How deep the spell wherewith she thralls,
  How wide her mantle is unfurled.

—Mary Clemmer.

Dusk is a sacred hour to nature. The little folk of the forest go a murmuring to their nests, the trees deal in gentle whispers, and even the capricious wind usually subsides. It is the hour of humility—the flaming monarch of the skies bids his subjects adieu and retires in regal splendor.

Know you the campfire at this hour? The first chill of the night air moves the circle closer, and the peaceful faces are lighted with the happy glow of the flames. The shallow amusements of daytime are no longer adequate, consciousness demands deeper joys. It is the hour of tenderness, meditation, reverent thoughts, and songs which come from the heart.

How surpassing brilliant is the evening star when it first sparkles in the afterglow of the western sky. How the swallows dart and dive in the still evening air, both for the food they gather and the joy they feel. How mystic the cry of the loon, the symbol of untamed nature, as he cavorts about the serene surface of the lake. How superior is the silent-winged hunt of the osprey as he glides in easy grace, silhouetted against the flesh-tinted sunset clouds. How sweet the woodland songsters as they strive to express the love and gratitude they feel for the gift of life.

Would you know the fullness of this hour? Be still!— as all nature stills to receive the invaluable gifts of silence. For the nonce, still even the voice of your thoughts that you may be wholly receptive. Let not the magnitude of the whispered revelations startle you; dare to indulge the most perfect of hopes. Abandon your egotism, release the love in your heart that has been withheld through self-consciousness, and let flow through you the grand and perfect ideas which are reality.

How restrained we are in accepting happiness. We hold back confirmation of love even to those we most adore. We hesitate to accept the joys of higher thought and expression lest it evidence some weakness or impractical strain in our make-up. We foster adversity by looking only on the sordid as reality. At times we seem more proud of our pains than our pleasures and darken the vista of life with morbid philosophies, rooted in egotism and fear.

The thoughts of the twilight hour do not rattle with armament and enmity. Do they then have less of reality? No, no! Accept them. "No hope so bright but is the beginning of its own fulfillment." Soar with the birds, scintillate with the evening star, sing with the sunset hues, and love with all creation. The flickering campfire in the slowly darkening woods is brewing heavenly thoughts which have been whispered throughout eternity—drink deeply!

There is a peace which settles upon the earth at twilight, not definable in terms of things and events. It is concurrent with the evening phenomena, not the product of them. It enters each unit of creation with healing effect, a soft light which illumines and guides all to a higher plane. Most of the consoling thoughts of the universe have crept into the consciousness of man in the sweet peace of the close of day.

Indian summer, the forest a riot of colorful splendor—
and feathered migrants are winging their way south.

WHEN THE RED IMPS PLAY

THERE came a night, still and cool, when soft opaque shades were drawn before the eyes of the world. Stars peeked through and sparkled with joy, like privileged few who could steal a look at the wondrous goings-on in the secret regions beyond darkness; for there were happy events in the making that night. All nature was atremble with expectancy. There was a smile on the face of creation and a twinkle in the universal eye, like the expression of a parent who has prepared for her children a surprise that is sure to bring ecstasy. It was not unlike the atmosphere of the night before Christmas when all hearts know that love is working miracles behind the thin draperies of secrecy.

Something was going on in the deep chambers of the forest. Something was afoot along silent shores and by the winding ways of streams. The very stillness that reigned was a happy delusion and a miraculous accomplishment in presence of that amazing activity which it concealed. For the very universe was seething with motive and motion!

And we, tiny tots in this immensity, stood on the shore at the fringe of this mystery, looking upon the shades before our eyes, wondering. We caught here a glimpse, there a sound, just enough to give hint of the half-hidden something that was going on, but never a full view—for nature can keep a secret.

Then came dawn, its sacred silence broken only by the singing of sunbeams. The spreading light of day swept all shadows back into the hills from whence they had arisen. A chill rested upon the atmosphere, pleasant to feel, as though it were joy in a new form. Then suddenly came the realization that a grand miracle had occurred, something of surpassing loveliness and grandeur had been brought to the plane of experience. Blue jays discovered it and raised loud their cries of praise. Crows carried the cry high into the heavens. Chickadees sang softly and incessantly of what they saw. Deer paused at their feeding, lifted their heads and stood as statues, spellbound at the spectacle before them.

We rubbed the sleep from our eyes, looked forth, then hurriedly rubbed them again, not quite willing to believe their testimony. For through the silent night the red imps had been at play with their paints, and before us was a world metamorphosed into a fairyland. Carnival had burst forth in riotous splendor. Such lavish costumes as adorned the forest that day—such ineffable hues. Such a bold blending of shades! Surely in all the

Autumn is not a sad season,
as some philosophy claims,
for life and joy abound
in the frosty air and festive hues.
Leaves drift to the ground,
not as a symbol of death,
but to enter a new role
in the uninterrupted growth
of the forest.

history of the world there had never been anything so beautiful before. Not a breeze stirred, for waters must be unruffled to act as mirrors in which nature might see its own attire. Creation seemed to stand still in happy amazement at the results of its endeavors, as though highest expectancy had been surpassed.

And those red imps—what happy imps they were. We could almost hear them laugh at our helplessness before this epic of beauty. Each way we turned, each direction in which we looked revealed new miracles. Comment was vain, and we could only sigh in humble appreciation. We were animated to keep moving, going —no doubt it was the red imps who led us on. They wanted to show us their work and to laugh at our bewilderment.

High on a hilltop they led us that we might look upon the ridges and ridges of scarlet-red maples. Down deep into valley and swamp they took us to show the rich yellow of tamaracks and the sly touch they have given to little ground plants. Out into groves of birches we went to stare up the pure-white trunks into sunbursts of yellow leaves; and on through measureless stands of aspens, dazzling in their orange hues, their leaves constantly dancing as if to say that were there no breeze they would make one. Along irregular lake shores we were drawn, and loud were the laughs of the red imps as we rounded point after point and bay after bay, each instant unfolding new breath-taking loveliness. Loosestrife trailed its rich, red tresses in the water, tiny birches and maples lifted their branches to say, "Look at us, we are beautiful too!" Oaks and elms, ash and sumac, alder and basswood, still but strutting, posed prettily as we passed. The very air itself seemed saturated with color—and the red imps laughed anew as we made this discovery.

Yes, the carnival had come at last, lifted to unprecedented grandeur. The red imps had been at play all through the mystery and silence of that night, extravagantly spreading their paint on everything that would hold even a drop.

And we could look upon this happy grandeur and love it. Well might we feel that we saw but a small portion of that which exists. There was much that was going on beyond our ken. Joy, happiness, contentment, worship reigned in the heart of nature. No doubt, in the midst of what we called silence there was music which we could not hear. No doubt, in the colorful patterns of foliage there were poems of unsurpassed loveliness, which we could not read. No doubt there was a prayer of praise on the lips of nature, which we could not know. No doubt there was promise and purpose to it all, which we could not understand. But at least we could see and adore—that was enough for now.

Can we not look upon
these lovely forest creatures
without plotting their destruction?
When we realize how empty
the world would be without them,
we shall be content
with the feast of beauty
and forego the feast of flesh.

❧ *PICTURES IN THE NIGHT*

We remember every precious moment of that beauteous fall evening. A full moon, barely above the treetops, illumined the woods. We made our way to Forgotten Valley, only a few rods removed from the road but separated by all infinity from the mad whirl of the world. The night air wore an edge of frost, which seemed objectified in the pale, white birches. Black moon-cast shadows, rich in mystery, lay in fantastic patterns on the leaf-strewn forest floor. The peace of endless ages rested on this tree-filled valley—a valley forgotten of men, but remembered of God.

Under the sheer mesmerism of quiet beauty we stood, still as the trees about us, imbibing the glory. Alert with interest and expectancy, our ears caught the sound of a cautious tread. It came nearer and nearer, till we held breath in anxious anticipation. Then before us passed a beautiful figure, so graceful and poetic it seemed unreal—a six-point buck! Hardly out of reach and happily unmindful of our presence, he came so close that we could see the luster of his horns in the moonlight and hear his soft, measured breathing.

No animal in all the forest was safer than he at that moment, for we had nothing to cast at him except awestruck admiration and love. And since then, amidst the clatter of cities, we have told of this experience to many openly envious of us—many who want to go and see him as we did.

Comes another picture. The moon has waned and night again grips the forest. A powerful motorcar moves slowly along the road which circles Forgotten Valley, its strong spotlight swinging rhythmically from side to side. The great buck peers forth from the underbrush, eyeing curiously this strange phenomenon which fascinates him and makes his eyes glow like burning coals. Within the big car there are excited whispers, a window is lowered cautiously, and a high-powered rifle leveled at the buck. Neither law nor license supports the plans of this "sportsman," but he has little use for either. The gun sights align on the noble gray head just between glowing eyes, and an anxious finger slowly presses the fatal trigger. But a sudden lurch of the car as it strikes a small rut disturbs the aim, and when the shot roars out in the still night, the buck wheels and disappears in the forest, followed by the curses of his would-be murderer.

And now a third picture. The great buck has been seen again, head erect, courageous, still undaunted. But his gait is no longer easy, graceful—no, and not painless. One beautiful leg hangs helplessly, the pitiful record of that shot that "missed." Every step is now labored, every jolt a piercing pain. His nights are filled with untold agony, his days with trembling fear. What a desperate handicap he bears for the stern battles before him, the ceaseless conflict with cold, hunger, and wolves.

O, Hidden Violator, what recompense did you gain in this sorrowful crime? Even if your shot had hit, and your overpampered appetite had been gratified, even if that beautiful six-point head hung mounted on your wall, what recompense? These many days we have been happy with our mental trophy, and the buck still at liberty to thrill others painlessly. But now, even now, he hobbles in indescribable torture, until some other in unintentional kindness comes with better aim. There are seasons for the slaughter; could you not have waited —given us the chance to see him once again?

There is something unfair, shamefully unfair, to the unoffending animal and to all the world in this.

Aurora borealis waves its mystic mantle across the northern sky and softly backlights the great woodland.

✒️ CAPELLA STOOPS
TO CONQUER

THE heavens are most friendly if we open our hearts to them. One is beautifully companioned, however much alone, when he may look aloft and call intimately by name the Pleiades, Orion, Ursa Major, Auriga. In the open spaces they counsel and guide; through the artificial lights of the city they reach down to inspire; and the very magnitude of their distances and proportions serves to enlarge and ennoble thought.

Man is a creature of sentiment, however much he struggles against it. No two things in nature hold the same degree of appeal to him. Thus it is that through sentiment we have chosen from the unnumbered legions of the heavens one star to call our own.

Capella, dazzling star queen of the north, first became enthroned in our adoration one perfect night on Basswood Lake some years ago. We were adrift in a gently rolling canoe, looking back at the captivating mass of limitless, black forest. A campfire lighted one small spot in the unbounded darkness, illuminating a ghostly-white tent, and we could hear the song and laughter of much-loved voices. The skies were aglitter with stars. Far to the southwest the horizon glowed faintly, and it gladdened thought to know that this marked the nearest approach of towns.

We had just remarked that not one thing could be added to deepen this beauty when our eyes caught sight of a star on the north horizon, barely above the jagged tops of the pines. It seemed in a frenzy of coruscation. Its very brilliance made it appear to leap about in a wild dance of joy. Its color changed from white to red, to green, to blue, faster than the words could be said. There was melody, rhythm, enchantment, regality in its performance, and though we knew not its name at the moment, we called it, "Queen of the North."

We watched the fair queen as she slowly swung to the east in her dancing and mounted into the upper heavens. She sobered as she climbed to her throne and assumed royal dignity. Her terpsichorean humor comes only as she drinks deeply of the wine of the earth's atmosphere. At the zenith she is adorned in courtly beauty, bright, imposing, but calm and aloof.

Capella never sets in the north country, but forever circles the North Star, attentive to her kingdom. Nightly she surveys her realm from her high throne—but then descends to mingle joyously with her subjects. Forty years is necessary for her lovely light to reach us, and it is well worth the waiting.

Our "Queen of the North" is a spectroscopic binary. The penetrating eyes of the spectroscope show her to be composed of two suns, one of which, in composition, is comparable to our own. These suns, endlessly circling each other, are widely separated, but at great distance they merge in appearance as one.

The skies boast no fairer child than Capella: not as bright as Sirius or certain of the planets, but more inter-eresting and varying in her queenly moods. She is a true northerner. At no time is her beauty in better display than as she dances in the gossamer of the Aurora. It is her nativity. The brighter the ghostly curtains and celes-tial beams, the more brillianty she scintillates. She toys with the pines, her silver image bathes in the still waters, she counsels and guides the wayfarer. A true empress is she, through beauty conquering a realm which adores her. Gladly are we enthralled!

A fairyland world greeted
this autumn evening!
Every tree trunk, branch,
twig, and leaf wore
a coating of fresh frost,
and ghostlike mists danced
on the placid waters. Nature,
with unimpoverished talents,
had produced a masterpiece.

MOON OF BARREN BOUGHS

THE carnival of autumn is over, though its dazzling brilliance still illumines the vaults of memory and the hills echo the wild joy of its finale. The red imps have had their day. They have established a new criterion of riotous beauty and virtuous debauchery. Thought will not soon relinquish the startling scene of the days just lived: the bold flashing costumes which adorned all growing things; the ineffable blue of the sky above; the happy mood of living creatures; the atmosphere of excitement that reigned; the sly yielding of nature to a moment that savored of frivolity, without the loss of dignity or poise. In that day of days when the festival reached its epic climax, each succeeding hour added beauty to beauty. Not a corner in nature or a niche in time was without some startling surprise from the whims of the red imps.

But there is potency to the wine of beauty. So much of it had been consumed that inebriation spread through the forest. Happiness grew to hilarity, joy broke forth unrestrained. The winds began to play a rhythmic melody in the pines, and the unseen, unheard, but deeply felt tom-toms of the red imps beat persistently. The music was soft, low, but syncopated and tempting, and the forest swayed to its rhythm. Once started, the spirit of revelry spread like fire. The north wind boldly raced through woods and glen, over hill and valley, down the course of streams, and across the surface of lakes, looking for any manner of musical instrument it might play upon. It made flutes of barren limbs, bassoons of caves and caverns, harps of pines and hemlocks, cymbals of lapping waves, trumpets of rubbing trees.

The forest swung wildly in the ever growing tempo. It flung its arms with abandon and flirtatiously toyed with the wind as it passed. Trees pelted each other with a confetti of their leaves, wild laughter and hilarious shouts filled the air. The last measure of dignity was abandoned. "On with the dance! let joy be unconfined!" Louder blew the north wind, wilder beat the red imps on their stirring tom-toms. Hordes of low flying clouds swept through the sky to look down on this carousing, and stars peaked between them winking at what they saw. Frost rode in with the night, but its chill presence only enlivened the revelry. And darkness drew its shades over the last scenes of this bacchanal—and perhaps it was just as well.

When the sun again rose, it looked upon a sober and sleepy-eyed forest. All through the woodland tem-

The queer but quaint opossum, with its bare prehensile tail, proves that nature has a flair for novelties.

ples were records of the Mardi gras. The forest floor was
half-knee-deep with confetti, whirled about and heaped
in piles by the momentum of the merriment. The north
wind still played its melodies, but the trees responded
little, wearily swaying their now leafless limbs. The party
was over, the mood could not be revived. Somewhere
in somber distance slept the red imps, their work for
the time ended, their purpose achieved. And the moon
of barren boughs was at hand.

But nature never knows aught that is inferior. Her
moods vary, but her beauty is perpetual, every accomplishment supreme. Her moments are not competitive,
not comparable. What she does this hour is the best
that this hour can know, but in the time that follows
will come that which is wholly different except in one
particular—it will be as perfect and beautiful in its place
as all that has gone before it. If in the moon of barren
boughs the forest is not so bright and sparkling as during
the carnival of autumn, it attains greater depths in
meditation and happy seriousness. In this time it is
learning things, reflecting, pondering, and it writes its
conclusions with barren branches—a lacery of hiero-
glyphs against the sky. Now it can digest the experiences of the year and thus be suitably prepared for more
revelation in seasons to come. This is the quiet hour,
the hour before nature draws over itself the white
blanket of winter and surrenders to repose.

It is not the time to be gay, though like all times it
is appropriate to happiness. Winds are becoming sharp-

edged and carry well the wolf howl. Wedges of wild geese frequently grace the heavens, their cries enriching night and moon; ducks dart like arrowheads that have flown away from their shafts; the last of the migratory birds are seeking the south. All creatures are using the wisdom given them by nature to make ready for whatever the unfolding future may hold. The woodchuck is already asleep, the bear is drowsy and looking for a bed, the chipmunk is putting final touches on his underground home, and the squirrel is storing cone, nut, and toadstool in well-placed caches. Forest aisles are thickly carpeted with leaves—the food factories of summer, the brilliant dress of autumn, the protecting comforter of winter. And all nature walks about with its finger on its lips that nothing be said or done to halt or hinder this moment of growth in understanding, the mood of meditation—the moon of barren boughs.

The fast 'flowing stream
never surrenders to the embrace
of winter. It laughs its way
out of the grip of freezing
temperatures and races on
in tunnels of snow and ice,
often the only voice heard
in the chilled solitude.

WINTER JUST CAME

WHEN the moon of barren boughs had waned and the world stood ripe for new adventure, there came a night that reached a new high in quiet. No breeze so much as strummed the pines, no leaf remained tardily aloft to weave its way with soft passing caress through the spider web of twigs and limbs. No whirr of wings, no cry of creature ventured to steal away that lively silence which ruled the chill, still atmosphere. Stars alone were allowed in the sky, for they know how to be quiet, and their light illumined hushed forest aisles. (Northern lights were perhaps forbidden lest their shifting beams snap and crackle, or their very motion suggest sound.) And gathering frost wove more and more intricate the webs of solitude.

We tiptoed to our cabin window and looked out into the night, for we felt a strange presence somewhere. A twig seemed to break, but we could not be sure we heard a sound. A tree seemed to creak, a leaf to rustle—

yet we could not say just where, or even if it were true. Starlight had the world under the spell of its magic: birch trees looked like concentrated beams of light that might vanish if approached; crumpled ferns were decked with jewels of frost; pine trees were like cut-out silhouettes against the sky; and distance was measureless.

We stared into this rich, cold gloom, striving to detect the something or someone we felt was there. But even as we watched, the strange presence laughed at our inquisitiveness and slowly drew a shade of clouds across the sky. The starlight gone, impenetrable darkness claimed the forest and nourished its mystery. Unable to see, we strove the harder to hear. There was something out in that blackened woodland, something wandering through those sylvan mansions.

(When thought has arisen to such poetic pitch it is impossible to know if that which it contemplates is something in the outside world or purely the invention of its own processes. Maybe there is another dimension of sight and sound which we attain in these rare moments.)

We seemed to hear a soft presence move across the leaves, but actual sound eluded us when we turned attention directly to it. Perhaps it was only the tresses of that star-cast cloud shadow. We thought we saw occasional flashes of mellow light, always at the left or right of extreme vision, but they were never to be found by direct gaze. Perhaps they were only moonbeam children detached and seeking adventure in this fairyland

The first heavy snow of winter
brings full the feeling
of wilderness to the north.
The forest is wild, free,
severe, vigilant! The voices
of wolves and coyotes ride
acrest icy winds, and the land
is laden with pure-white glory.

world. Several times we heard human voices, and though this is an old and favorite trick of nature, we found ourselves momentarily taken in.

Then came a little hole in the cloud curtain, and a handful of stars hurriedly peeked through, their twinkling smiles lighting up the world just enough to give it momentary form. Hastily we glanced about to find objects solid and tangible. There was everything in place —the lake, great bodies of trees, distant shores, island, points, and bays. And in the air were pinpoint sparkles that looked like flaked moonlight, floating particles of pale phosphorescence—or was this again some trick or illusion? But we had only a moment to look, for the rip in the cloud curtain was quickly drawn together, and utter darkness ruled once more.

Now the something in the forest moved again. We could hear it tread upon the leaves, a sound as soft as the fall of dew. It brushed against trees like the touch of a spider web upon a cloud. It moved across the water like the singing of starlight on fields of snow. It crept through brush and shrubs like the passing of time in the land of dreams. And we went to sleep, leaving our thoughts detached and wandering in this realm of lovely fantasy.

When daylight came, we hurried to the window to see if there was anything to identify our visitor of the night before. One look and we could not fail to know what it was. Telltale tracks were everywhere—the white, clean tracks of winter! It had stepped upon the leaves, covering them with its footprint of light snow. Where it had brushed against the trees, snowflakes had been left in crevices of the bark. On twigs and branches were clustered evidences of its passing, and the grasses along the water's edge had turned to crystal at its touch. Joy and good cheer filled the cool air that morning, and the sun sang as it looked upon and gathered up the evidence of winter's first visit.

What a multitude of memories our hearts can recall—
memories more precious to us than the treasure of kings.

✑ FROZEN MEMORIES

THE heart-warming gratefire wearies of its flames and subsides into a softly glowing bed of coals, its waving radiation re-creating priceless dreams and memories. Let no other light dim this glow which casts grotesque, dancing shadows on the cabin walls, yet illumines the very chambers of meditative thought. There are pictures playing on the screen of embers, cherished pictures which the power of Mammon could not buy.

Beneath that fallen log, whose ends still grip the andirons while its center falls to coals, lies a scene once thought forgotten. A canoe glides through long stretches of white water, its paddlers tired by hard travel. They swing precariously near to subsurface reefs, scanning always the rock-bound shores with anxious eyes for a spot to camp. But it is a rugged country and campsites are none too numerous. They move out on the open waters of mighty Lac le Croix just as the sun dips its lower edge in the liquid horizon.

Next they strain tired muscles to meet a stubborn head wind, striving to reach the far shore before darkness doubles their difficulties. What these shores hold they know not, but trust they are more friendly than the ones left behind. Daylight pales, the waters blacken, the evening star braves the afterglow—still the measured swish of paddles and the search of anxious eyes.

Now an island looms before them, bearing all their hearts' desire! A campsite, a stone fireplace, ready-hewn tent poles, rock-dried moss and balsam for their bed— their kind has been here before. They make a fire, cook the bacon and the coffee; no monarch ever dined as they. All the labor of the day is forgotten. Aurora is dancing in the north sky, meteors streak the heavens, a wolf calls in the distance; the campers add fuel to the fire—life is too full for sleep. Wrapped in blankets they watch the embers, burning red-orange, until they glow like these in which this picture lives. Then—

Where the night went they never knew, for in an instant it is dawn, and another day upon them.

In that coal near the backlog, fringed with white ashes like the first sweet touch of advancing years, lies the image of one perfect day. It is high noon and a gentle, cool north wind balances the heat of the sun. The sky is a superlative blue, intensified by one lovely, lazy white cloud—all living again on the quiet surface of the lake. How white the birches on this day. How joyous the gentle play of aspens. How deep the green of

The campfire's ruddy glow warms hearts, rests harassed minds, nurtures friendship, and refreshes hope.

pine and hemlock. Martins coast and dart through the air, redwings sing, perched on swaying reeds, and from some hidden forest chamber comes the unmatched song of the hermit thrush. High the hawk circles, while through ferns and logs dart the little things of the woods. Not a day for high adventure, just a day to live and love.

In that mass of embers where tiny blue flames play lies a memory near too sacred for words: night, afloat on placid waters, so still we seem suspended in the midst of a sea of stars. Not a motion—we just sit in spellbound wonder at the sphere of miracles which we center. Then comes a moment of supreme stillness. Even the canoe ceases its drifting, and all nature stands in reverent expectancy. The eastern sky lights with transcendent glow, and over the serrated treetops slowly rises the full moon, "fair mistress of the night." Night birds call their greeting; a whippoorwill swings through the headlands to awaken all to see this wonder; fish leap high for better view; and the great chorus of frogs chants its lay.

We move on with silent paddles along the ghostly shore. A buck stands in the shallows feeding, his antlered head held high. He is a statue carved from the moonlight, a lovely spirit of the forest, unafraid though the canoe drifts two paddle lengths away. We sit motionless, scarcely breathing, until the frost-air chills our fingers, and a paddle slips with alarming crash on the hollow canoe. A snort! A flash! The deer is gone, laying a trail of fading sound through the darkness. All night long we cruise the shores, gathering eternal treasures, till the gray shows in the east. How glorious that such sacred memories can never be taken from us. What a blessing that life's greatest riches are beyond reach of time or decay!

The embers burn low and my heart rests in dreams. Far, far north the white waters, lakes, woodland flowers, and trees, all lie silent under spell of winter. Frozen memories!

But tomorrow the magic rays of the sun will warm them to life, just as the glow of the gratefire has this night quickened them in thought. And who shall say that they were more real in that hour when first lived than in these fireside meditations? They are now enriched by understanding and endeared a thousandfold. If dreams stir hearts and thoughts and lead us into deeper love, are they not another phase of reality?

The mere owning of a cabin
does not make it home.
We must live in it,
work and play in it,
people it with loved ones.
We must seek it for shelter
from storm and strife,
make it the throne
of our best moods,
the seat of happiest hours.

✒ *HUT HAPPINESS*

GREAT as is the treasury of joy held in the limitless vaults of the outdoors, it is not a monopoly. The captivating charms of forest trails, emerald waters, and wild-wood friends, furred and feathered, could be recited without end. They never disappoint and never surfeit but, through years of association, constantly grow in appeal. Yet while gratefully adoring this unfailing source of joy and beauty, we should not fail in appreciation of the sweet happiness of the cabin fireside.

Hut happiness has entwined in it both the practical and the ideal (if these be distinct). It symbolizes protection, security, and comfort. It is the seat of love and the throne of tranquillity. All other joys seem, in a manner, to grow out of hut happiness, for along on the journeys into the forest one carries the sweet assurance that he will return to the fireside, to protection and comfort. The cabin is the starting point and the objective of every plan.

The very heart of hut happiness is the fireplace. With what peace we recall the picture: a favorite chair, a loved book, house slippers, and a moderate gratefire with a few sticks of cedar to give it voice; muscles comfortably tired by an active day. Out in the night it is raining, beating a staccato dance on the thin roof. Trees lash before a stiffening wind—each sound making the Sanctuary more dear. Silence and peace. Our eyes close for a moment as we think gratefully of each loved phase of our environment. We think of the fireplace, of the pattering rain, the great forest, and the black waters of the lake now streaked with white foam—then again of the fireplace. Time was when the fireplace was merely an object of utility, when the function of its rays was to give physical warmth, but it has attained a more spiritual purpose. Loved ones are dearer by firelight, dreams are sweeter, plans are more noble, faith is strengthened, hope is surer, and truth is apprehensible.

Hut happiness is inextricably interwoven with friendliness. What greater delight is offered man's soul than the contemplation of a circle of happy, friendly faces, lighted with the glow of the gratefire. The evening is alive with wit, song, and laughter—remember? There is a beautiful familiarity in the freedom of this atmosphere, which renders us conversationally superior to our wont. The conventional mannerisms which bar intimacy and discount sincerity in most gatherings are happily absent here. We are natural as the trees, unsophisticated as the skies. Neglect no ritual in this evening of delight:

It seems incredible
that the fantastic patterns
of frost on a windowpane
are the mere concurrence
of crystallized moisture.
One imagines an invisible
artist recalling the type
of foliage used in ages past,
or designing some anew
for time to come.

the ceremony of popcorn, toasted marshmallows, broiled bacon; the frankfurters and the inevitable coffee made at one side of the coals. Hunger does not call for these, they are a pageantry of good-fellowship.

Often in the north-woods sojourn (too often for some) comes the lazy day. But the occasional lazy day is a joyous part of hut happiness. One wants just to lounge about, sit on the porch, and look out through the trees and over the lake; he wants to do nothing that demands of him special decision or energy. With what fine resourcefulness the cabin meets his wishes and caters to his mood. There is the swing on the front porch which creaks out a musical drone as he sits and looks aimlessly about, enjoying all but thinking of nothing. There is the friendly book ever at hand, yet unoffended if one's interest in it is brief. There are the daily papers, a month old, still entirely new and interesting. There is the neglected list of correspondence; some hooks to sharpen and boots to oil. If the day grows warm, perhaps energy might be stirred to take a brief dip in the cool lake and then enjoy a siesta. The lazy day is a lovely part of cabin joys, but guard against its lures—to be beneficial, its frequency should be limited.

The charms of hut happiness are never more vividly expressed than when written on the snows of a winter evening. Approach the cabin after a day on snowshoes— tired but happy, cold but hopeful, and with an appetite that is all but dangerous to fellow men. Look on the nearing cheery light of the windows as it lays a brilliant pattern on the pure-white snow. Warmth, welcome, invitation seem to burst forth from every crevice. Loosen the snowshoes with numbed fingers, enter this haven, pull close to the fire, and catch the tantalizing odors of the dinner in preparation. How the hands and feet tingle and the cheeks glow as the blood again warms and circulates! What a sense of ease creeps over you as you relax—rest. (Oh, there is a vast difference between natural tiredness and the nervous exhaustion of the competitive world!)

No power on earth could move you from this comfort, save the dinner call. And no barrier of politeness or conflicting ambition could hold you thereafter from the inviting bed. How the whole cabin seems to wrap about you, while outside nature crackles with cold, and the chill beams of the moon light a fantastic pattern on the frosted windows; and over a trail of dreamless sleep you make your way to another day.

Man is a home-loving creature, the nomads of his race are few. It is only when he views things in the light of home that he perfects and respects them. As his dwelling is home, his neighborhood, his city, his state, his country, even the world is home. Were man not so sensitive to the soulful appeal of hut happiness, society would have made no strides toward higher civilization.

Deer feeding on a winter landscape;
snow-covered balsam trees,
serene beneath a gray-blue sky;
a drifted, velvetlike white carpet,
made dazzling by the sun—
the north country prepares
for Christmastide.

CHRISTMAS SCENE

WE ONCE looked upon a spacious spruce swamp at Christmas time and there gained a criterion for all landscape beauty. We were snowshoeing through pine-covered highlands in the north when a valley opened suddenly at our feet, as if a spontaneous creation. At once we christened it "Surprise Valley," after the manner of its discovery, and later retained the name because of its resourcefulness in ever revealing new charm.

A prehistoric lake had carved out this fairyland. The ancient shore line was still clearly defined. Through unrecorded years the waters had silently and secretly sought the sea, leaving their vast saucer-shaped home to nature's next phase. The great basin became a sunken garden carpeted with soft sphagnum moss out of which had sprung legions of lowland spruce—perfect of form and charming of character.

"The universe is a thought of God," wrote Schiller. How glorious must be that infinite Intelligence which

conceives the thought that is this valley. What orig-
inality of setting it offers for the Christmas scene, what
startling composition, what daring contours and bold
combinations. Our use of trinkets and tinsel on our
ceremonial trees is but inadequate plagiarism.

Stand with us as we again look into this basin of
beauty. Forget the limitations of time and space while
we contemplate nature in her most reverent mood.

Each conical spruce, capped with new snow, is a
pyramid of crystalline purity. Our eyes are met with the
brilliant sparkle of unnumbered jewels. Look! That
seeming immobility is but an illusion. The valley seethes
with movement. Stupendous ceremony is under way.
As far as the eye can reach hosts of white-robed spruce—
angelic choirs—march rhythmically without motion, sing
divinely without sound. The tread of the devout legions
is softened to silence in the moss-padded aisles now
doubly cushioned with the symbolic white carpet.

What mute joy fills the air. Birds flutter from limb
to limb like incarnate notes of the sacred theme; a deer
paws the snow away to nibble at underlying mosses; a
squirrel feasts on a spruce cone and sprinkles the white
earth with the crumbs of his repast. No part is super-
fluous, no part is lacking. The scene exemplifies the law
of synchronized events—the eternal and unbroken pro-
cession of predestined causes and inevitable effects.

The spirit of giving reigns and at our feet we find
gifts unspeakable. Wrapped in the mood of the moment

we find *humility* wherewith we clothe ourselves to be worthy of this adventure. We find *reverence*, *hope*, and *faith* among our precious presents and feel the dawn of an instinctive understanding of life's deep secrets. Our hearts are filled with *beauty* and *joy* that glow within us cheery as a Christmas hearth. We learn a lesson in *giving*—for this giving is not bargaining as is sometimes true of the gifts of men. These parcels come adorned with love and labeled by the hand of Him who saith, "All that I have is thine."

Nearly two thousand years have elapsed since the Prince of Peace came to lay before benighted humanity his revelations. We are only beginning to understand some of his teachings. But we are coming to see that not only on one day of the year should we commemorate his birth by practicing his principles, but on every day. The wisdom he spoke is ageless. He came "not to destroy, but to fulfill!" He brought us no new earth or heaven but revealed to us the glories of that which we already have.

Jesus of Nazareth saw the hand of his Father in all nature and turned to the silent mountains and wilderness to refresh his spirit and pray. He preached the power of love and kindness in a world that was proud of its hate and cruelty, he placed not even a sparrow or a broken reed beyond the scope of his doctrine. He brought into consciousness a new sense of values: "It is the spirit that quickeneth; the flesh profiteth nothing!"

But of the ceremony: the legions of marching trees sway with a gentle breeze, soft snow lightly sifts to the ground as if frozen light from invisible candles. Louder and louder grows the anthem of spiritual tones, far sweeter than any sound.

Then of a sudden comes a great hush! The marching hosts of trees halt. The sun is overshadowed by a cloud. We stand atremble. Is it the cold, or the sheer, spiritual magnitude of our experience in this realm of poesy? What is this hush—is it the end? Have we seen all we may?

No, it is but a pause to accentuate the supreme climax. The sun suddenly bursts from behind the cloud, its glory magnified a thousandfold. Clouds blush crimson at its touch. Surprise Valley is flooded with a golden glow. The massive choirs are again in motion, their song reaching the very heavens. They are retiring into the gathering shades of evening. They troop over the hillside, they march through crevasses of the ancient shore line. The sun dips below the horizon, seeming to pause for one last look into this fantastic winter world. Twilight obscures the last acts of the sacred rites. The vaulted dome of the cathedral lights with the first stars of evening. Night comes on in filmy purple robes and all nature bows head in long, silent prayer.

Cheeks aglow, toes atingle, still under the spell of the vision, we move homeward to the measured swish of snowshoes. Venus hangs like a lantern at the western horizon, Sirius scintillates in the eastern sky, the constellation Orion beautifies the zenith. We hold back all conversation, for each knows that the other is striving to fix permanently in thought our experience— that strange and beautiful blending of fact and fancy, that union of the inner and outer worlds, that oneness of thought and nature we have seen in the Christmas spectacle of Surprise Valley.

Streams are flowing freely,
swollen with melting snows;
the sun sends its warm rays
right through frigid winds;
buds are swelling; and there are
familiar cries in the heavens.
The year has run its course,
spring is here again!

FROSTY STEPS TO SPRING

THE longest stretch of winter in the north country comes after Christmas has been wrapped up and neatly stored away. Now follow three months when temperatures are lowest, storms are hardest, and the face of nature most austere.

Comes January, long of evening and cold of day, a month of flickering fireplaces and pensive meditations—wavering betwixt memories and plans. Lakes are locked in rigid sleep, forests cloaked in white mantle, wild creatures face their sternest days, yet beneath the cold is the promise of joy to come. Sap is poised for its springtime journey, while in the frozen ground the arbutus and trillium are primping for their early debut. January, in thy frosty hands is held the seedling of the year!

Comes February, and winter attenuates. It becomes translucent, yes, even transparent. Spring lies behind the thinnest of veils. Even the zero blasts come in new, warm luster. Venturesome birds, prophetic scouts of migratory hordes, slip silently into the scene. A new brilliance adorns the sun's rays, and whatever the temperature, the surface of the snow melts at their touch. The fireside holds the body, but thoughts reach afar. Now plans become preparations. The peak and pride of winter is February—frosty of breath, yet warm of promise. Thenceforth, though storm and chill linger on, all is a part of spring.

Comes March, like a cherished old grandsire, a grumpy beloved for all his idiosyncracies. He caresses one day and chastises the next. He coaxes the tulip through the thawing earth with the smile of spring, and then chills it with leftover winter winds. He entices the sap to the end of the twig, then pinches it playfully with frost and sleet. He opens a day with the blue skies of June and in a twinkling coats them with charging clouds of gray. His breezes are fitful and deceptive, sometimes playing about the barren branches of deciduous trees and leafy limbs of pines in lazy wafts, sometimes raging through the forest in cyclonic revelry. He loves to hold a blizzard or two in hiding; then just when we have put our winter trinkets away, he heaps the land high with surprise snowdrifts and sends us scurrying after snowshoes, sleds, earmuffs, and such things again.

But we will not be deceived! We know beneath his pretense of eccentricity March is a dear old soul, a friend to all the year. We know in the legacy of his melting snows and torrential rains is growth and development. Let him rant and rave, we will see his true worth and laugh at his feigning. We will look beyond his troublesome tricks to the glorious evidence of spring that breaks through everywhere. Then some day when he has exhausted his pranks and departed on the way to another year, we shall meet April again, with a wreath of spring beauties in her hair.

INTO the pages of this book is woven anonymous reference to many treasured friends who have wandered the Sanctuary trails with me, compounding the experiences and working out the philosophy herein presented. I am deeply indebted to them. I wish also to mention specifically the valuable assistance and photographic contributions of Grant Halladay (pages 10, 19, 28, 56, 61, 70, 92, 95, 108, 114, 146, 156, 180, 212); Art Merigold (page 177); William F. Rubert (page 140); Ted Tadda (pages 67, 98, 150, 184); Staber W. Reese and the Wisconsin Conservation Department (pages 38, 47, 64, 85, 88, 119, 134, 159, 162, 166, 174, 200); Frank Gehr (pages 73, 76, 105, 111, 153, 191); John Szarkowski (page 122); W. C. Carson (page 194); J. W. Jackson (page 44); and my beloved wife Virginia Campbell (pages 14, 22, 33, 50, 82, 102, 128, 170, 188, 197, 206, 209, 218).

S. C.

PRINTED IN U.S.A